MW00799584

What Others Are Saying About This Book

She knows what the heck she's talking about… This Author emphasizes the need to have an approach that is laced with empathy and understanding... taking into context the past and recent traumatic history of a client/person being served. …I will recommend to my peers and associates. Don't hesitate.... add this to your arsenal of resources and buy yourself a copy right away! – Caz and Cassandra, Consultant

I loved the simple explanations to very complex issues. Theresa's combined personal and professional life experiences are practical and heartwarming! – T. Turner, Advocate

This book really changed my perspective on thinking of what trauma is. I use this title "Its Not Drama it's Trauma" in a lot of my workshops now that I have a full understanding that everyone story can have a sense of trauma and we can't disregard them until we know the history. So, if you would like another perspective, get this book ASAP. – T. Easley, MHFA Instructor

As a former foster youth and someone who has worked in higher education with probation and foster youth, this book really explains the whys of behaviors and situations. "IT'S NOT DRAMA, IT'S TRAUMA" speaks of how trauma affects the body and how we as educators can address foster youth and probation youth with empathy, understanding, and compassion. This is a great tool. It also has practical tools you can use in order to engage and encourage the youth. Theresa, you did an amazing job at writing the book!!!! Kudos – E. .Henderson, Former Foster Youth

I think that this is a very thought-provoking book. The information itself is highly informative and helpful. I think that the personal information that you put into the book illustrates that you genuinely care, and it gives you a different insight that others might not have- J. Berry, Editor

The effects of trauma on the life of individuals is a serious matter and I think the client population served by DCFS would be interested in what Theresa has to share - J Kerr, Social Worker

It is especially important to have resources unique in helping individuals who have experienced trauma. I am interested in utilizing evidence-based practices shared in this book to assist those who have experienced trauma. - A. Jones, Therapist

I've worked with children that have gone thru trauma...The book will bring knowledge and understanding to the effects of trauma. - Y. Williams, Caregiver

It is dynamic, exciting, timely, and relevant. The book highlights the need for understanding the social impact of this important topic. – S. Wilson, Guardian Scholars program staff

It's Not Drama, It's Trauma

By Theresa Reed, M.Ed

A Guide to Empathetic Trauma-Informed Engagement with Foster Youth for Higher Education Professionals

ISBN: 978-1-941749-90-6

LCCN: 2018908720

May 2021

Promotional Access

Thank you for purchasing *It's Not Drama, It's Trauma*. You have now joined an elite group of professionals, caregivers, and advocates dedicated to improving the lives of children, youth, young adults, and adults who have experienced the foster care system.

Please send us an email or visit my website. As a thank you for purchasing the book, please visit my website to access:

- a free download of the e-book
- exclusive access to worksheets
- a free thirty-minute consultation on implementing trauma-informed principles within your agency
- discounted workshop fees

Books are available for purchase through several online bookstores: Amazon, Barnes and Noble, Goodreads, and Google.com. It is also available in our online store at www.INDITstore.com.

Best wishes,
Theresa Reed
Website: **www.traumacollaborative.com**
Email: TheresaReed@outlook.com
Follow me on social media:

Like and follow me on social media:
@itsnotDramaItstrauma or
TheresaTraumaReed
@itsnotdramaits

Table of Contents

Dedications

To my mom, Barbara Jean, you gave me life and the strength that has made me the woman I am today. I love and miss you!

For Papa, the rainbow, the only father I have ever known. You quietly loved, encouraged, and supported me. Thank you for my introduction to business and teaching me that "I wanna tata you" is another way to say "I love you."

Ganna, for you a delicate, long-lasting flower. You have always said, "Give me my flowers while I live." Thank you for being my flower and believing in me.

To Mr. Arthur Jackson, my mentor, who knew me before I knew myself. Thank you for being my educational muse. Although you were the school psychologist, you were my friend and inspiration.

Thank you to all my families, friends, and past, present, and future "loves." Your presence in my life has shaped the experiences that give me the inspiration to share myself with others in the pages of this book.

To those who doubted me, discouraged, or talked against me, thank you for motivating me to achieve my dreams and defy the odds!

To my pride and joys, the apples of my eye, my children: Tatiana and Amani. You have been a constant source of love, motivation, and wonderment. Thank you for teaching me and for providing me with a living classroom.

To Gramanie's Angel, La'Rell, I love you!

Foreword

As a State Senator and a former state Assembly- member, I have been fortunate to have the opportunity to meet with thousands of people and organizations during my ten years in the California State Legislature. At each meeting, I have had the privilege to learn about the good work being done to improve the lives of others, as well as the critical need to address developmental issues. My meetings were filled with information sharing: statistics on the problems or issues, stories of those affected, and ideas on how to tackle problems. These meetings provided me with the tools I needed to develop policy proposals or legislative interventions.

Throughout the years, I have always made sure to author legislation that addressed gaps of service in the foster care system and higher education. With the help of people like the author of this book, Theresa Reed, I have been able to ensure that siblings have visitation and interaction, that IEPs are expedited for youth in high-level placements, and that Cal Grant funds are earmarked for youth.

Within the pages of *It's Not Drama, It's Trauma,* you will find a toolkit rooted in the author's own story through foster care, her journey through education, and ultimately her experience in developing client-centered programs. This book contains a piece of her, which allows for the growth of empathy and understanding of a youth's experience, and also serves as a reference guide you can use to learn and develop the skills necessary to serve youth while understanding *It's Not Drama, It's Trauma.*

Anthony J. Portantino
California State Senator, 25th District

Acknowledgments

A special thank you to Coach Laura Brown for creating SWOT Book Camp, for inspiring me and providing me the tools to finally birth this project.

Thank you, Corri, for the push and the introduction to Coach Laura.

Thank you to Deb McCurdy and Jessica Berry for your patience and diligence in editing.

About the Author

My Story: That Was Then

How are Michael Jackson, Teena Marie, thirteen, and a brown leather case related? They all are remnants of my time in foster care. On the last day of school during my seventh-grade year, my mother picked me up from school and told me we were going to the house to pick up my sister. We entered the side door of the house like we always did, but things seemed different. My sister had not arrived yet, and I saw none of my other siblings—I did not even get to say goodbye to them.

I went to the room my sister and I shared. I do not remember if I was told to pack my things or if my belongings were already packed. I do remember the one thing that even remotely resembled a suitcase— my record player. Clothes were no big deal to me. Most of my outfits were hand-me-downs from my sister.

The record player was in a brown faux snakeskin case and had been a Christmas gift. No one else in the house had one, so I cherished that brown leather-like case along with my copies of the albums *Triumph* by Michael Jackson and *It Must Be Magic* by Teena Marie. Michael and Teena helped me through the many lonely days that I would experience.

Unlike many children in foster care, I am fortunate that I only lived in two placements. After spending the "longest summer ever" in my first foster home in Los Angeles, I was moved back to Pasadena to return to my school district of origin. I will tell you more about my first placement in the next chapter. For now, I want to highlight my time with the Brockmans, Papa and Ganna.

As a child, I felt welcomed into their home, and people could not tell I was not an original member of the family. I am thankful to Papa and Ganna for the love and life lessons they shared with me. Papa introduced me to business by letting me help with paperwork for his construction company. Ganna taught me to bake and took me to open my first bank account.

At age fifteen, the judge asked me if I wanted to return home. I said, "No." Firstly, I believed if I had returned, I would have become a teen parent. I saw too many examples of poverty breeding early pregnancy. As the third of my mother's eleven children, I decided I did not want a lot of kids. Secondly, I believed I would have lost my spot at the Brockmans' home. Their maximum age was thirteen, and I was already fifteen. If I left and experienced the inevitable failed reunification, I could not return. My third belief was I would have become the built-in babysitter at my mother's house. Most of the time at the Brockmans' home, I was an only child. Why would I want to return to living in a house full of little kids? My last belief was I would not have graduated from high school.

In the second grade, I met my educational muse, Mr. Jackson, the school psychologist. He saw talent in me and encouraged me to stretch my limits. I wanted to emulate his educational success by attending his alma mater, the University of Southern California (USC). Eventually, I attended USC to begin my doctorate.

I cannot say these beliefs would have become a reality, but I am glad I did not take the chance. I remained with the Brockmans after I emancipated until I thought I was "grown enough" to get married at twenty years old.

My Story: This Is Now

I was one of those different kids who liked school and learning new things. My mother suffered from sickle cell anemia. So, I missed days from school to stay home and take care of her. It bothered me to miss school. After I went into foster care, I required a doctor's note to miss school. The belief that education was my key to a different life permeated many of my choices.

Unfortunately, there was no Guardian Scholars Program staff, like you, to support me in pursuing a college degree. Yes, I floundered a bit. Immediately after high school, I attended a vocational school. I knew it would take at least four full-time minimum wage jobs to take care of myself, so I needed some skills to make a livable wage. I also knew I wanted to get a degree and I could not ask my mother to write a check for college tuition. I planned to make enough money to afford to pay for college.

I did not know anything about the FAFSA (Free Application for Federal Student Aid), or fee waivers.
I was taking one class at a time at Pasadena City College for two years before I learned about FAFSA from a friend. Armed with this information, I attended California State University, Los Angeles where I completed my Bachelor of Arts in Economics. After a ten-year "break", I completed my master's in education at the University of

Phoenix (UOP) thanks to a full scholarship from The National Foster Parent Association. The Friday before my Saturday graduation ceremony from UOP, I received an email from USC informing me I still had a chance to apply if I completed my application within seventy-two hours. My initial response was, "What, with all the celebrating I planned to do, how am I supposed to finish by Monday night?" Well, I did it and completed one-third of the doctoral program. Then life happened.

In 2013, I experienced a series of life events which derailed my education. I was diagnosed with a life-threatening pulmonary embolism while I was overseeing two full-time work assignments. While in recovery, I took on the adventure of buying my first house. These are all things they suggest you avoid if you want to be successful in the program. I have since re-enrolled in my doctoral program.

Currently, I work for Pasadena City College as the Program Director of Foster/Kinship Care Education (FKCE) and the Student Advisor for the STARS Foster Youth Program. I am no stranger to pioneering foster youth support programs. Within my twelve-year tenure, I helped found our Guardian Scholars equivalent, STARS, and convened the first regional Foster Youth Success Initiative (FYSI) in 2009. I have had the good fortune to oversee several life skills program subcontracts. While wearing dual hats managing FKCE and coordinating Journey to Wellness through the Student Mental Health grant in 2013, I received certification as a Mental Health First Aid Instructor. For over fifteen years, I have been facilitating workshops for various colleges, K-12 districts, the Department of Children and Family Services, and multiple conferences, including the Foster Youth Education Summit and Blueprint for Success.

As the John Burton Foundation was entering the arena of providing technical assistance to colleges, I contracted with them to consult with five Southern California colleges in developing their emerging foster youth support programs. Most recently, I cowrote our CAFYES/Next-Up application. As if I do not have my hands in enough pots, I created the STARS Resource Centers, which are now operating weekly at six local K-12 schools.

I could provide more details (and yes, there are more) but do not want to bore you, plus I have limited space. You might be thinking, "Wow, that's already a lot." Those of you who are veterans of foster youth support programs are aware that it does take a lot. Those of you who are a novice, consider this a foreshadowing, but know the effort is worth it. This summary of my experiences is intended to "convince you" that I have been traversing this terrain for some time and might be able to share some things with you that may find useful.

~ *Theresa Reed*

Preface

Even though trauma is something serious, I like to infuse a bit of humor in my presentations. My children think my style of comedy is corny, but they laugh at it anyway. I do not know if they are laughing at me or with me, but I continue to use it.

I have many stories and analogies to share but cannot include them all in this first book. So, stay tuned for more in the subsequent additions.

Why I Wrote This Book

It's Not Drama, It's Trauma is a guide to help those who are interested in being empathetically trauma-informed when engaging with children, youth, young adults, and adults who have experienced foster care. It is practical, interactive, and humorous. Many agencies proclaim they are "trauma-informed," yet are unable to show evidence of practical application. I am not a mental health professional, but I am an educator, advocate, and former foster youth desiring to help others heal.

It's Not Drama, It's Trauma will be a series of books addressing the unique needs and concerns of various audiences. I decided to start with the college foster youth support programs because this is where I got my start professionally and gained much of my knowledge. There has been a surge in awareness and resources at higher education institutions. I wanted to be at the forefront of the expansion and provide a tool that would go beyond face-to-face workshops and conferences to aid you in the work you do. Rest assured, the book will not replace me, and I am available to work with you and your partners to enhance the lives of your students.

While much of the focus in this book is on students, I have not forgotten you as the professional. I also encourage you to practice self-care by being trauma-informed about your own need for healing from trauma.

How to Use This Book

My style of presenting information is to make it as plain as possible. I do not want to add to the stress you may already be experiencing as a professional working with students.

I provide plenty of subheadings in the table of contents. So, you can quickly navigate to a topic you feel is most relevant or interesting, although I think it is all exciting and relevant.

The structure of the book is also intentional. It is mixed with research findings to support my ideas, analogies from the field for practical application, and activities to increase your learning. Within each chapter you will flow through four major elements:

1. **Sharing my story** - Here, I am taking the opportunity to be vulnerable and share pieces of my personal story as an emotional appeal to illuminate the topic we are about to discuss.

2. **Defining it** - We often use words out of habit but have not examined what they mean. I have become a walking dictionary. In this element, I break down terms and share research or data to illustrate the information from a more scientific viewpoint to validate my assertions.

3. **Connecting it** - I will use analogies and scenarios to sway an empathetic view of the chapter topic.
4. **Applying it** - I present activities for you to complete. These activities are to encourage you to reflect on or practice the knowledge gained in the chapter.

Additionally, I have sprinkled "Suggested Trauma-Informed Responses" throughout the book to provide immediate alternatives to some scenarios. These are boxed and labeled "STIR".

I do hope you enjoy taking this journey with me. My learning objectives are that you:

1. Gain a deeper understanding of trauma.
2. Learn practical ways of applying the trauma-informed framework.
3. Develop an empathetic approach to engaging with students, bearing in mind their experiences in foster care and how it manifests in adulthood.
4. Utilize knowledge gained from this book to build resiliency in students.
5. Recognize the need for self-care to reduce vicarious trauma in yourself.

This version of *It's Not Drama, It's Trauma* is intended for those working with foster youth in a college setting. However, the information provided on trauma, its causes, the long-term impact, and strategies for positive engagement can be informative or useful to anyone and even foster youth.

Let the journey begin!

1

Drama vs. Trauma

In a conversation with a colleague who has worked with group homes for years, she shared a heart-wrenching episode she witnessed. Her agency also serves as an emergency shelter facility for all ages. Staff was escorting a young boy to his new room after completing the intake process. En route to the cottage, he ran from the path and began scaling a fence to escape. As staff reached for him to pull him to safety, he screamed, "I just want to go home; I want my mommy!" To an unwitting observer, this child was being dramatic. After all, he was being protected from an abusive situation by being placed in a state-approved, safe group home. So, why would he want to go back to an abusive situation?

My Story—My First Day in Foster Care

How is a 12-year-old girl supposed to respond when her mother asks her, "What do you think about going into foster care?" After the emotional response of shock passes, a few colorful responses may come to mind like, "Why the heck would you ask me something like that?" There is no role-play scenario you can share with a child to prepare for this conversation. My response was, "Um, okay." I knew enough that no matter what my answer was, my mother already had an irrevocable plan in motion. So, on the last day of seventh grade, my mother dropped me and my sister off at the Pasadena office of the Department Of Children and Family Services (DCFS), which is on the same street that serves as the route for the Rose Parade.

I guess the county code requires all facilities to use the sterile white paint on the walls and to buy the cold steel gray metal desks. This environment was so cold and impersonal (not trauma-informed). I remember the matching coldness of Barbara, the social worker. I have never been arrested but talking with her that day made me feel like a criminal. I suppose in some ways I was and had been sentenced to "life" without the possibility of ever being the same again.

Barbara did not make eye contact and did not ask if we needed anything. I sat in a chair, watching her shuffle papers for what seemed like hours. I remember her mumbling something about the trouble we had caused my mother then we were off in her car. There was very little, if any, conversation before she dumped me and my sixteen-year-old sister at a house in South Central Los Angeles. For a nerdy, skinny girl born and raised in Pasadena, this was like going to another country.

Defining It

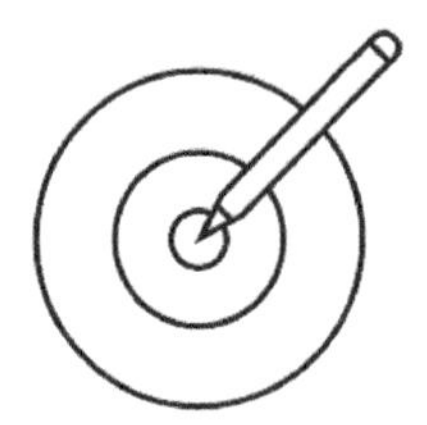

Trauma has an impact on everyone. If you experience a traumatic event, it will manifest in your actions and behaviors. You may avoid people and places that are reminders. If you work with someone who has lived through something traumatic, the manner in which it is manifested will likely impact your interactions with them. They may appear oversensitive or you may have difficulty engaging them. This may cause frustration or may appear as an unwillingness to comply, just as the little boy in the opening paragraph for of Chapter 1 appeared to be non-compliant. The appearance of unfamiliar behaviors may cause someone to interpret the actions of others as being "dramatic" when in fact, it may be a natural response to some known or unknown trauma.

What Is Drama?

Since the title of the book is *It's Not Drama, It's Trauma,* before I can talk to you about what trauma is, I need to discuss what drama is. It is important to provide clarity on what is and is not actually the result of trauma. The dictionary defines drama as "a way of relating to the world in which a person consistently overreacts to or greatly exaggerates the importance of a benign event." Typically, "drama" is used by people who are chronically bored or for those who seek attention. This definition is not consistent with the behaviors of a child who is thrown into the world of foster care.

If a student told you, "I am terrified to stand up and make a speech in front of a crowd," would you tell them they were being dramatic and to get over it and go do the speech? In the midst of an advisement or counseling session, if a student declares, "I do not really want to tell you about what I've been experiencing; you're not going to understand and there's nothing you can do about it!" would you think they were being dramatic? What if a student has a meltdown and "goes off" at the front counter after being told to go to three different departments and is still not getting the help they need with their financial aid? Is this student being dramatic?

When you understand the long-term impacts of trauma, you will have greater empathy for some of the behaviors described above. Let's examine the situations I just listed:

1) The student terrified to give a speech: While this may be a normal feeling you can relate to, perhaps the student was embarrassed horribly in a previous situation so now they avoid it altogether.

2) The student refusing to talk to you in a counseling session: Unfortunately, many students in foster care have had years and years of therapy. In their perception, it does not help if they are still experiencing the same kinds of things.

3) The student going off at the front counter because of problems with their financial aid: An initial response might be, "Just calm down: we can figure this out" or, "It's not so bad. The payment will come later." These are not comforting responses for someone who is in survival mode. For many students, financial aid is the only steady source of income they receive. Something as routine as a delay in financial aid processing could be a trigger reminding them of being homeless or a previous history of deplorable living conditions. To them, their basic survival is at stake.

So, for someone with developed coping skills or a support network for when things go awry, these kinds of situations do not appear to be life-threatening. For a student who has lived with many distressing experiences without a consistent adult to help them navigate or problem-solve, these seemingly small or routine occurrences represent extreme events which require extreme responses. Now that I have shared a glimpse into the perception of drama, let's examine what trauma is.

What Is Trauma?

Trauma is an emotional or physical response to a deeply distressing or disturbing event. What is considered distressing or disturbing is relative. The event could represent direct harm to you or an act which threatens the life or physical integrity of someone close to you. These events are known as traumatic experiences. One absolute is that trauma leaves a mark on all of us. When you experience a physical threat, you have an emotional response. This experience impacts your brain whether you were hurt or not. Your brain reacts the some either way.

Types of Trauma

1) Acute Trauma
2) Chronic Trauma
3) Complex Trauma

Acute Trauma is a onetime, random occurrence, such as a car accident or witnessing violence. Have you ever been in a car accident? Because of the accident, do you now do something differently when you drive? Perhaps, you no longer drive a certain route. Maybe you leave more space between you and the car ahead of you, or have you stopped driving altogether? This onetime traumatic experience caused your brain to go into survival mode to avoid re-experiencing this distressing event. Interestingly, what we ultimately default to is the original information we learned in the student driver's manual which was designed to promote safety and survival.

A onetime event, such as a car accident, is enough to cause a shift in your behavior, your feelings, and your relationship to other people. You may not ride with the person who was driving anymore or no longer allow the person to be a passenger in your car because they were a distraction. Even your view of the world may be altered. Now your thought is, "Nobody knows how to drive" or "Nobody pays attention." As a result of this onetime experience, a piece of your brain is reshaped and says, "Hey, we need to do something different, so we do not experience this ever again."

Chronic Trauma is repetitive trauma, happening at some regular interval. This may include combat situations or domestic violence. Imagine a child who has witnessed abuse or domestic violence. You might read a report and say, "I do not see in the report any physical evidence of abuse, so why am I seeing evidence of trauma?" A child's emotional reaction to what they witnessed triggers their startle response, and their body does not know the difference as to whether it is happening to them directly or to someone else. After experiencing a series of traumatic events or chronic trauma, the brain goes into long-term survival mode.

Complex Trauma is Chronic Trauma occurring at the hand of a trusted loved one. Foster children suffer from Complex Trauma. How are you to navigate life when the adult who was supposed to explain that there is no bogeyman under the bed or that it doesn't even exist was, in fact, the bogeyman. Who does the child now go to for help making sense of life's "stuff"?

Have you ever witnessed a car accident? You might have awakened the next day with some unexplained soreness. The reality is, your body reacted by tensing up as if you had been in the accident you witnessed.

Here is what happens when you have been exposed to a traumatic event:

- You feel an overwhelming sense of terror, helplessness, and horror.
- You experience intense physical effects such as a pounding heart, rapid breathing, trembling, dizziness, or loss of bladder or bowel control.

These reactions ignite your startle response, also known as the fight, flight, or freeze response.

Have you ever had the pleasure of being the guest of honor at a surprise party? What reactions did you have in your body when you opened the door? Were they anything like the symptoms listed in item two above? Probably. You may have even had one of these reactions:

- **Fight**: taking a swing at whoever was standing in front of you
- **Flight:** run out of the room
- **Freeze:** stood there and could not move

Hopefully, you did not experience the loss of bladder or bowel control as you stood there frozen. If you did, I have a secret to put you at ease. What you experienced was the body going into survival mode by lightening the load in preparation for flight. When the startle response is engaged, the body reacts as if you were being chased by a two-ton bear—in the moment, it does not know the difference between a bear and a surprise party. The reactions are all the same.

No matter what trauma you experience, it affects your behavior, feelings, relationships, and view of the world in profound ways. It causes you to go into survival mode. When you are in survival mode, your other senses are not so sharp. You are not attuned to emotional cues, you are not trying to make new friends, and you are not trying to learn the 3Rs—reading, writing, and arithmetic. Being in survival mode for a prolonged period now becomes your normal state of being, which impacts your ability to learn new things or trust new people.

For a child in foster care, a life of abuse is like being in a car accident or having a surprise party (not in a good way), or being chased by a bear every day of their lives.

Suggested Trauma-Informed Response

If someone tells you, they do not like surprises or do not like celebrating certain occasions, please do not force your ideas on them.

Unfortunately, abuse is often associated with commemorating special days. Sometimes our well-intended efforts can retraumatize someone we care about. Letting the person know you accept their view can be comforting and help to build trust.

S

T

I

R

Reactions to Trauma

Excess hormone production

Let's take a closer but basic look at the startle response. When you get startled, the brain releases a surge of hormones. The two primary stress hormones are adrenaline and cortisol. Adrenaline increases the rate at which the heart pumps blood to the muscles to get them ready for running or flight. The companion hormone, cortisol, increases the production of glucose for the muscles to use as fuel. During this production, cortisol temporarily immobilizes other systems like digestion, growth, reproduction, and the immune system. When a bear is chasing you, what's more important, eating or running? The startle response makes this decision for you. For an athlete, activation of these chemicals heightens their performance.

Both adrenaline and cortisol have a role in daily functioning. However, too much of either can cause damage. If the body continues to produce adrenaline, it can cause damage to the heart such a high blood pressure or even heart failure. Excess cortisol levels are associated with weight gain, anxiety, and sleep disturbances. Additionally, too much of either chemical in the brain can erode its surface causing permanent brain damage and resulting in mental disorders. There is no way of knowing which part of the brain the chemical can destroy. Later in the book, we will discuss what the brain might look like when a person suffers from a mental disorder.

Causes of Trauma: Physical and Emotional

"Sticks and stones may break my bones, but words can never hurt me." Whoever wrote this adage was certainly not trauma informed. As a child, I was taught to recite this phrase as a countermeasure to the hurtful utterances from others. No matter how many times I'd repeat it, it did not make the words hurt any less. You cannot unhear things. You certainly cannot unhear hurtful words spoken to you by your mother.

My Story: Sticks and Stones May Break My Bones

One Saturday afternoon, I was eagerly awaiting a phone call from my mother. After what seemed like an eternity of waiting, I was finally on the phone with my mommy! We engaged in small talk about how I was doing, where she was living at the time, and how my siblings were doing. Somehow, the conversation took a strange turn. I do not recall the specifics. Maybe I asked a question that struck a nerve. I really do not know. What I do recall were the last words spoken to me by my mommy on that day. She declared, "I hate you." I broke into uncontrollable tears. How do you respond to such a statement? Especially if you do not know what you did wrong.

I am thankful my foster mom was listening in. She gently took the phone from me and ended the call. To this day, I do not like to use the word "hate". It makes me cringe when I hear people use the word in a joking manner. Speaking maliciously can be more damaging than physical abuse. What my mother said hurt worse than the time she whooped us with a mop handle which broke after she hit me. It hurt even worse than landing on my head after flying off the teeter-totter at age nine.

It does not matter if the traumatic experience was physical or emotional. The residual effects of either can be equally detrimental.

Physical causes

A fall or hit to the brain can cause bruising or irreparable damage. The knowledge that a person's brain was injured because of a blow to the head invokes a greater level of sympathy, empathy, and understanding. The two examples of physical causes prevalent with foster children I will highlight include brain injury and Fetal Alcohol Spectrum Disorders (FASD),

Brain Injury

Helmet laws were created for a reason. Research has shown that the brain is particularly vulnerable to injury on impact. So, maybe you encounter a student who struggles with short-term memory or has demonstrated an inappropriate emotional response when frustrated. You learn a student has sustained an injury during an accident. You respond, "Oh, now I understand why they are acting 'differently': their brain was hurt in the accident because of the injury they sustained." This is a logical outcome from the injury. Human nature compels you to be a little more patient or even make concessions. You might go as far as scheduling an appointment for them to be assessed to receive accommodations. This type of injury is very pronounced and obvious. Injury from FASD is not as obvious and often misunderstood.

Fetal Alcohol Spectrum Disorders (FASD)

Fetal Alcohol Spectrum Disorders is a group of disorders that are a result of the mother's use of alcohol during pregnancy. Effects from exposure can manifest as physical problems or problems with behavior or learning. However, they are usually a combination of these problems. When a mother drinks alcohol during pregnancy, it has a traumatic effect on the unborn baby. Picture an adult who has had too much to drink and how it affects the brain: their speech is slurred; they have a hard time walking on their own; their cognitive ability is impaired, making it dangerous for them to drive; and they may even have a lapse of memory. Now imagine the effect on the undeveloped brain of a fetus from consuming alcohol in utero. Prolonged usage may cause lasting damage and may affect a child in any number of the following ways:

- Abnormal facial features, such as smooth ridge between the nose and upper lip
- Shorter than average height

- Poor coordination
- Hyperactive behavior
- Difficulty with attention and memory
- Learning and intellectual disabilities
- Poor reasoning and judgment skills

Figure 1: Facial Features of Child with FASD

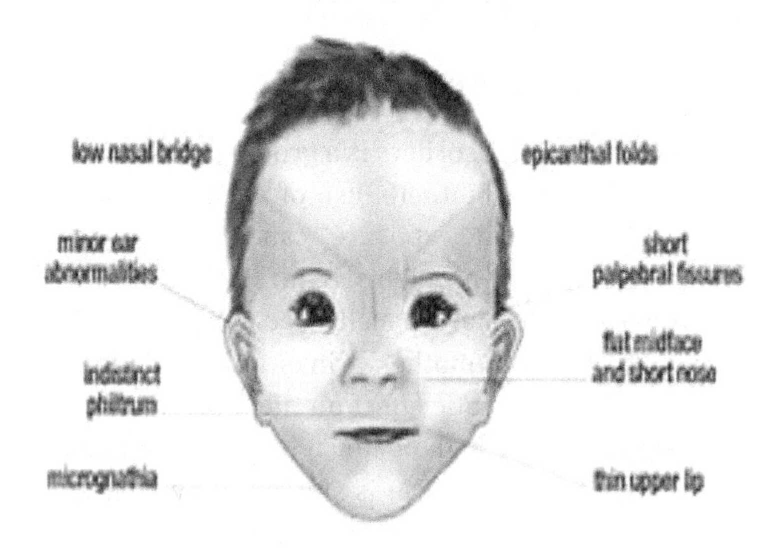

Unfortunately, alcohol kills brain cells. Some of these effects may not be apparent until adolescence. During adolescent development, the brain is supposed to transition from child-like thinking and behavior into adult critical thinking, reasoning, and problem-solving. Children with FASD are unable to make this transition because thc original brain stems did not even have a chance to grow.

Here is an analogy for those of you who enjoy gardening. It would be equivalent to planting flower seeds, watering the seeds, and waiting for them to germinate in anticipation of transplanting them to your outdoor flower garden. You now set an automatic timer for watering, knowing it should take about three months for this phase. After the requisite eighty to ninety days, there is no trace of a blooming flower for you to transplant. Devastatingly, you cannot complete your garden. Just as not seeing the physical changes you expected can be a big disappointment, the aftermath of emotional abuse can be equally devastating.

Emotional causes

If you cannot see a scar, does it mean you are not hurt? Oh, if only this were true. Emotional abuse is harder to prove but it happens and is just as traumatizing as physical violence. Here are some scenarios when someone is being emotionally abusive:

- The use of shaming or belittling language
- Constant criticism or attempts to manipulate and control
- Withholding affection
- Threats of punishment
- Isolating someone from supportive friends and family

Causes of emotional abuse include neglect and insecure attachment.

Neglect

Let's play a game of True or False. Is this a form of neglect?

1. Not feeding a child regularly?	True __ or False __
2. Limiting or withholding hugs and kisses?	True __ or False __
3. Ignoring conversation or continually being unavailable?	True __ or False __
4. Missing regular medical checkups?	True __ or False __
5. Allowing a child to miss an excessive amount of school?	True __ or False __
6. Not tending to a crying baby?	True __ or False __
7. Poor hygiene?	True __ or False __
8. Improper use of medication?	True __ or False __
9. Not being encouraging after a person does a good deed?	True __ or False __
10. Not allowing a child to socialize with others?	True __ or False __

If you answered "true" to all ten, then you are correct.

When a child's needs are not being met, they are being neglected. Unfortunately, neglect leads to what is called insecure attachment and ultimately, lack of trust. Neglect or insecure attachment is a form of trauma and trauma affects attachment. There is no winning situation when neglect is at play. Neglect leads to feelings of insecurity.

Insecure Attachment/Distrust

Let's look at the Cycle Of Attachment and how it works.

Figure 2: Cycle of Attachment

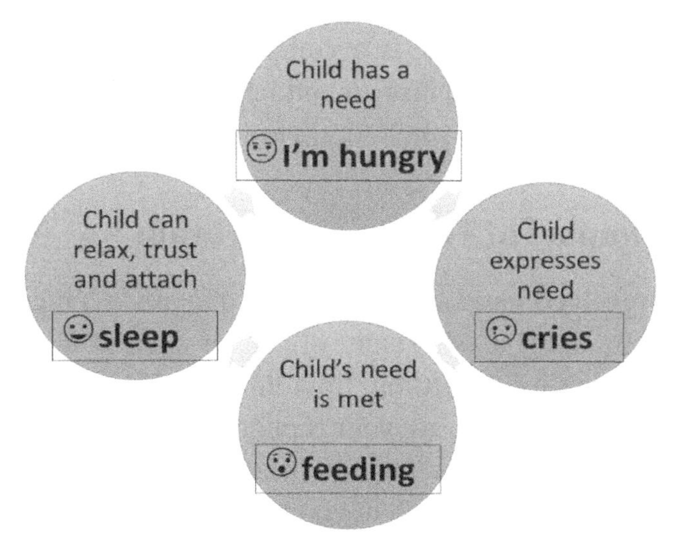

From the visual depiction in Figure 2, here is a scenario of a toddler. They are hungry, so, they have a need to eat. Crying is usually how they express the need. In a healthy situation, their primary caregiver meets the need by feeding them. Once they are fed, the body begins to relax. They are no longer crying. They burp, relieve their bowels, and are ready to fall asleep. When this cycle flows

properly, the child and caregiver are attaching or building a bond of trust. The caregiver's responsiveness to the child's need, lets the child know they can be trusted. Child can relax, trust, and attach.
Where there is trust, there is bonding.

Conversely, with insecure attachment, if the need is neglected, the child is unable to relax and learns to distrust. The child is still hungry and is then forced to seek other means to have their needs met, such as cry to someone else, eat whatever they can find, or adapt to doing without. This severe neglect is traumatic and forces the brain to alter its process. Neglect of any kind impacts physical, emotional, and psychological development. Attachment is a complex issue. Trauma disrupts attachment and insecure attachment is a form of trauma. This disruption alters brain functioning.

Impact of Trauma on the brain

You just received news that your schedule must change to accommodate a shortage of office space. This adjustment can be unsettling. How does this make you feel in your body? What are your thoughts and actions in the moment? Perhaps, you felt a sensation that could be described as a surge or rush in your brain? It feels like a valve has opened a little wider and extra liquid came in. The body is a finely tuned series of automated processes. What you may have felt is the release of cortisol and adrenaline. The sensation I described is the result of neurotransmitters sending signals to prepare you to respond to a potential danger and keep you safe because the brain senses distress. Figure 3 shows the systems that are activated during distress.

Figure 3: The Corticolimbic System

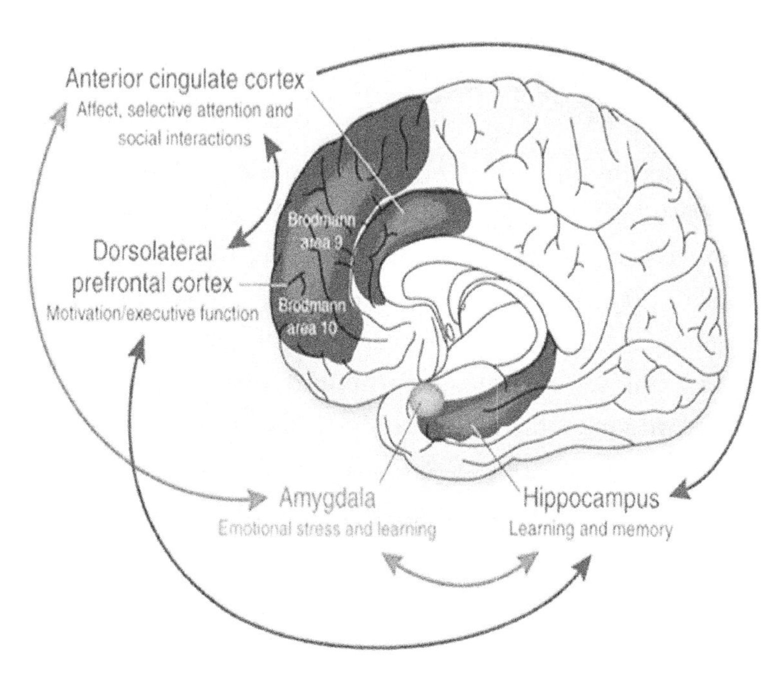

During a stressful situation, the limbic system (the hypothalamus, the amygdala, the thalamus, and the hippocampus) is activated, leading to the release of the stress hormones cortisol and adrenaline (Fig.3). These chemicals have a specific destination, a specific time frame to get there, and regulations on how long they are to remain there. After performing their duty when the brain signals "all clear", we are safe, and they get released back into the body. If either chemical stays in the brain too long, it's like having your toilet back up, resulting in damage to other systems. In other words, the brain must recalibrate other systems to handle the excess, potentially overworking other areas of the brain. Some resulting damage may include excessive worry, hypervigilance, avoidance, or extreme moodiness. Figure 4 below, is a more scientific look at the systems and their areas of responsibility.

What It Looks Like

Please pardon the inner "Amy the Neurobiologist" in me. The brain is a fascinating mechanism. While this section is a bit more technical or even text-bookie, I think it is important to include this information as we are defining trauma and its impact on the brain. In a question and answer session with some current and former foster youth, the conversation was heavily focused on mental health and the misuse of psychotropic medications. One student had a brilliant solution. He declared that every foster youth should have a scan of the brain performed before they are diagnosed and prescribed medications. This is my attempt at honoring his request. So, let's dive into the inner workings of the brain.

Figure 4: Parts of The Brain
Listed clockwise as the names appear in Figure 4.

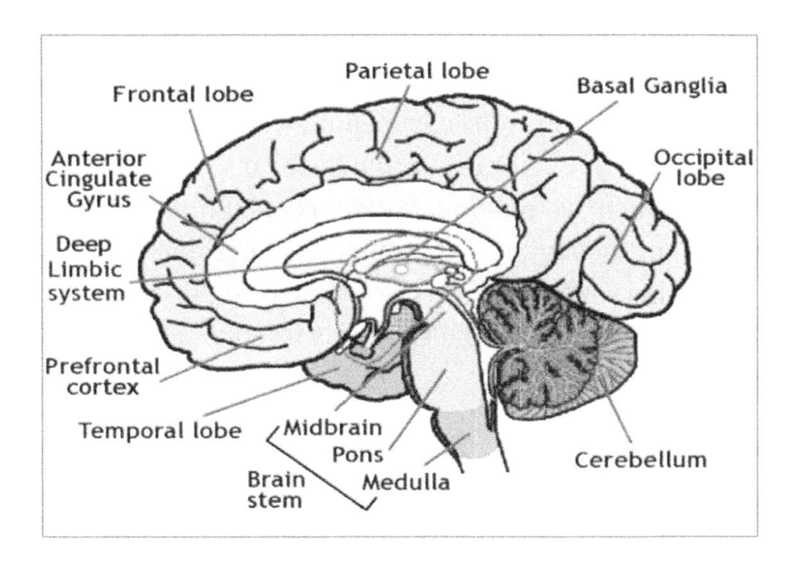

Cerebral Cortex. Although it is not labeled, is a thin layer that covers the four lobes and the cerebellum. It is responsible for:

- Determining intelligence and personality
- Processing sensory information and language
- Motor function
- Planning and organizing

Brainstem - The brainstem is a collection of three areas of the brain. These parts are the **Medulla**, **Pons**, and the **Midbrain**. The brainstem is located below the cerebellum and connects the brain to the spinal cord. It has the job of running all the involuntary muscles. These are the muscles you don't consciously control, such as the muscles which make your heartbeat. Together, these three parts of the brain help keep us alive by controlling our breathing, digestion, and blood circulation.

Temporal lobe houses visual memory (such as facial recognition), verbal memory (such as understanding language), and interprets the emotions and reactions of others.

Prefrontal cortex sits directly behind your forehead. This area of your brain provides for executive functioning, such as making decisions, planning, and adjusting your behaviors according to experiences or cues from others. When this area of your brain does not work as it should, your life falls into disorganization and behavioral problems.

Deep Limbic system (the hypothalamus, the amygdala, the thalamus, and the hippocampus) effects emotions, memory, sensory processing, time perception, attention, instincts, autonomic/vegetative control, consciousness, and actions/motor behavior.

Anterior Cingulate Gyrus regulates heart rate and blood pressure and is vital to cognitive functions, such as reward anticipation, decision-making, empathy, and emotion.

Frontal lobe coordinates high-level behaviors, such as motor skills, problem-solving, judgment, planning, and attention. The frontal lobe also manages emotion and impulse control.

Parietal Lobe receives and processes sensory information. The somatosensory cortex is found within the parietal lobe and is essential for processing touch sensations.

Basal ganglia control voluntary motor movements, procedural learning, routine behaviors, or "habits" such as teeth grinding, eye movements, cognition, and emotion.

Occipital lobe is heavily involved in the ability to read and recognize printed words, along with other aspects of vision.

Cerebellum is the part of the brain that is responsible for human movement, coordination, motor control, and sensory perception.

Where It Is Affected

Now that we have dissected the parts of the brain, I would like to connect the dots between extreme alterations in mood and the parts of the brain responsible for the range of activity that we see manifested in behaviors.

Brain Scan of Person with Anxiety Disorder

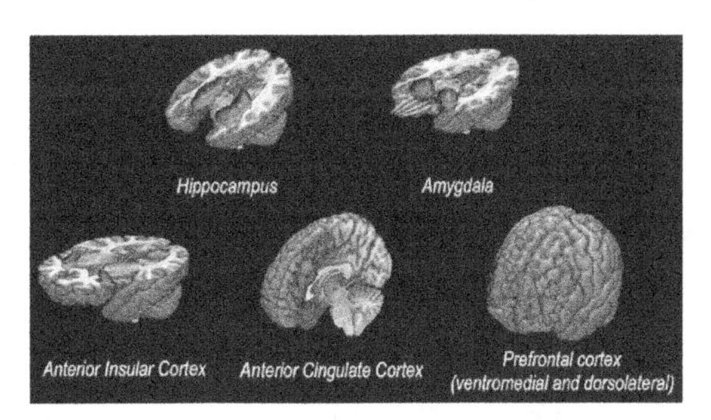

Excessive worry looks like a decrease in activity of the pre-frontal cortex, anterior cingulate gyrus, and hippocampus of the limbic system, for a combined effect of dysregulation of emotions, heart rate, and cognitive functioning. Simultaneously, elevated activity in the basal ganglia, manifests as diminished control of learning and body movement i.e. jitteriness. This prolonged activity leads to anxiety disorders.

Brain Scan Comparing Normal Brain to Person with PTSD

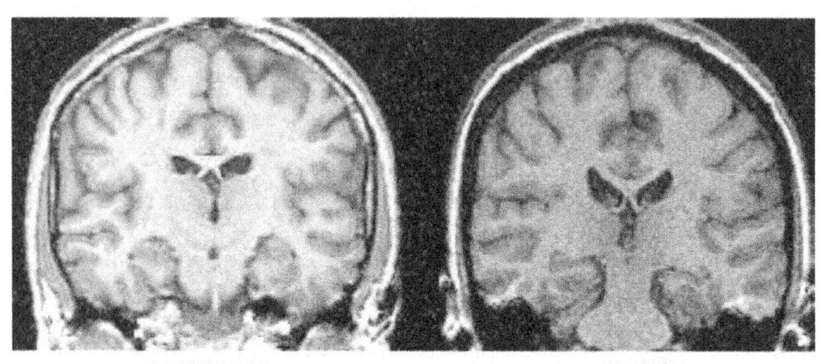

Hypervigilance in the brain shows up as increased activity in the anterior cingulate gyrus (hyper-focus) and in the basal ganglia (anxiety). Additionally, there are some abnormalities in the right lateral temporal lobe (recognizing and reacting to others). Excessive exposure to these conditions translates into Post Traumatic Stress Disorder (PTSD).

Brain Scan of Person with Reactive Attachment Disorder

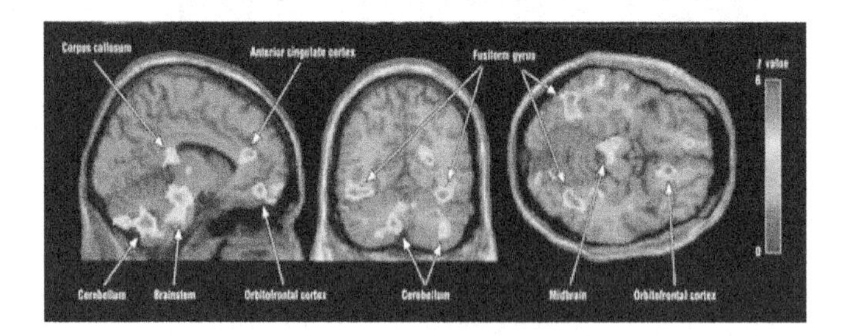

Avoidance is a survival response to trauma. Would you continue to expose yourself to people or situations that cause you hurt? You wouldn't do so intentionally. Continuous sensations in your body caused by hurt effect activities in your cerebral cortex, resulting in avoidance. These negative hurtful sensations can lead to issues with trust and attachment, or what is known as Reactive Attachment Disorder (RAD). As you can see from the picture, there are a lot of areas beneath the cerebral cortex that are affected.

Brain Scan Comparing Normal Brain to Person with PTSD

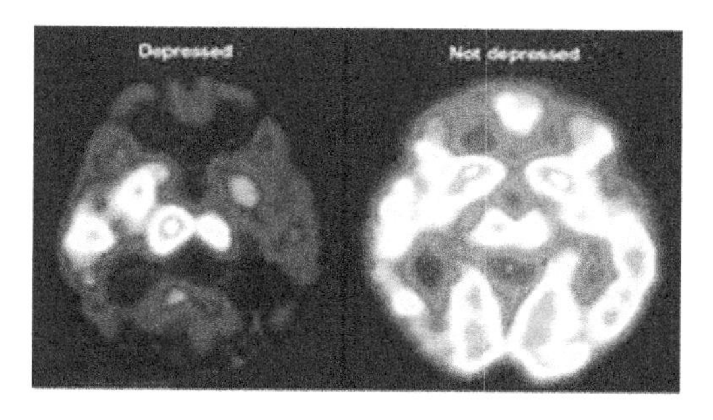

The extreme moodiness associated with depression may result from elevated activity in the deep limbic system which processes emotions. You can see from the picture the areas that are affected appear to be brighter. Depression is characterized as prolonged episodes of negative emotional states such as restlessness, irritability, feelings of guilt, worthlessness, helplessness, or hopelessness, and sleeping too much or too little.

I chose to highlight excessive worry, hypervigilance, avoidance, and extreme moodiness because these are among the common behaviors I have observed, and which my colleagues have shared, as most concerning in our work with college students from foster care. This is but a small list of potential damage to the brain caused by trauma.

Connecting It

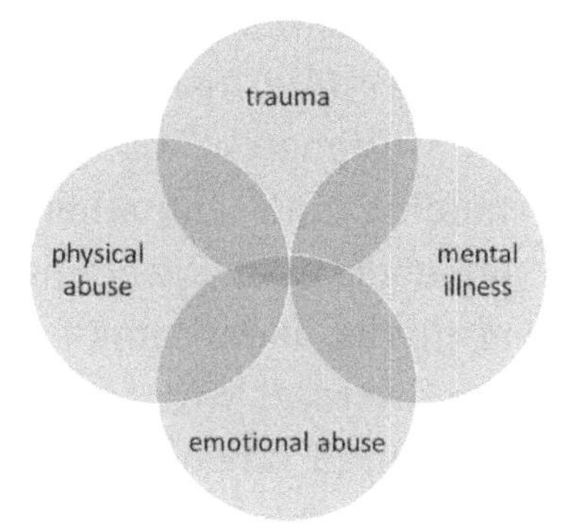

As promised, I shared with you some definitions around drama vs trauma and potential causes. I think the brain is such a fascinating "machine." I hope you too were enlightened by the details I provided on the parts of the brain and their functions. Let's transition to the next element by connecting all of this background knowledge into ways trauma may manifest in the long-term.

Prolonged exposure to stress affects the brain in a variety of ways. In the short run, the startle response causes the body to gear up for fight, flight, or freeze. This response is okay. It is what the body is designed to do. However, when the body is constantly aroused by distressful situations, the brain reprograms and reshapes itself by staying in survival mode. Survival mode is supposed to be a temporary condition, not a state of being. When the brain remains in an altered state of functioning, this may signify mental illness.

Mental Illness

What is mental illness? This is the jackpot question. As a Certified Mental Health First Aid Instructor, I am often asked this question. Unfortunately, many people are much more understanding and empathetic when it comes to physical ailments. In my training classes, I spend time dispelling myths and stigmas around this concept. I would like to dissect it with you. Simply put, mental illness is the impaired functioning of the body part which is responsible for thoughts, emotional state, and behavior—the brain. Mental illness does not discriminate. One in six people are dealing with a mental health issue but many are not seeking help due to stigma and discrimination.

College Statistics On Mental Illness

- Forty percent of the nation's young adults between ages 18-24 are enrolled in college.
- Onset of 75% of all mental illnesses occur before age 27.
- Less than 20% of college students with a diagnosed mental disorder are receiving services.

In 2012, I had oversight for the Journey to Wellness Program. During this program, students from Pasadena City College were among the 14,000 respondents to the nationwide survey on student health. I was particularly interested in students' perceptions of factors which negatively impact their academic success. Figure 5 highlights findings from the survey.

Figure 5: Student Reported Negative Impact on Academics

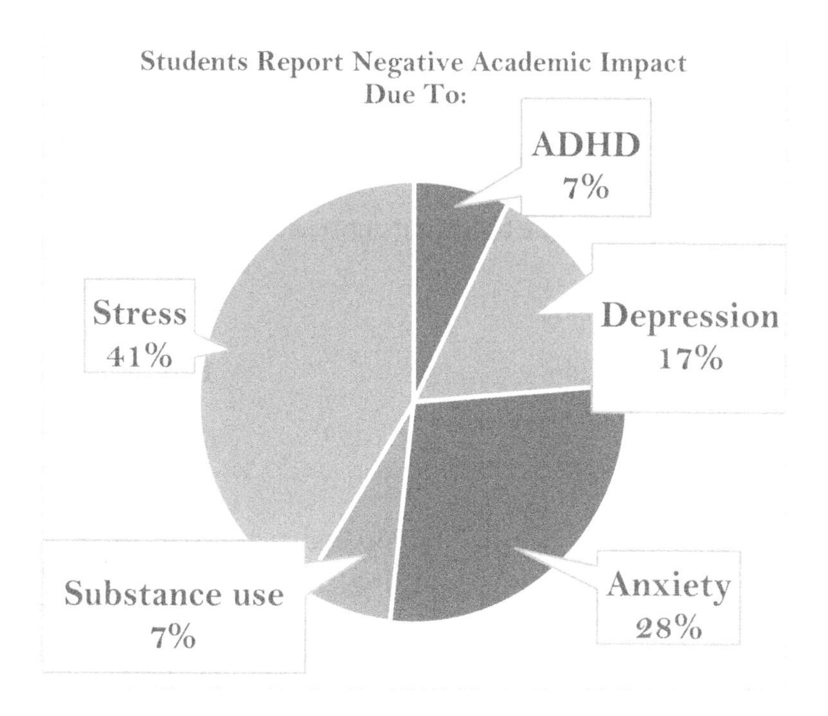

The graphic above shows student reported mental health factors that contributed to challenges with academic performance. Stress and anxiety were present more often. Additional data in Table 1 below shows the percentage of students reporting feelings of hopelessness.

Table 1: 2014 Student Report on Feeling Hopeless

felt hopeless	44.6%
felt very lonely	56.6%
felt overwhelming anxiety	49.9%
hard to function due to feeling depressed	29.5%
considered suicide	6.9%
attempted suicide	1.2%
self-injured	5.5%

As a Certified Mental Health First Aid Instructor, I use this data to enlighten others regarding the prevalence of mental illness among college students. Mental illness does not discriminate. Additionally, having a childhood history of trauma, as is the case for foster youth, puts students at greater risk for a mental health diagnosis.

Common Disorders in Foster Youth

Raise your hand if you have ever been angry. What are some things you do when you are angry? If it is easier, think about what your "friend" does when you, oops, "they" are angry. Do they/you:

- Yell
- Throw things
- Ignore
- Walk away
- Drink
- Stress eat

If these specific behaviors were examined in the context of symptoms of mental illness, they might be associated with the following disorders:

Yelling: Tourette's

Throwing things: Aggression

Ignoring: Selective Mutism

Walking away (withdrawing): Depression

Drinking: Substance Use Disorder

Eating: Eating Disorder

Many foster youth are very angry because of the forced separation from their birth family. While they may understand there was abuse (there are scars), it is not explained why they must be taken away from their parents, siblings, friends, bedroom, or even their house. Depending upon how the anger is expressed, foster youth are labeled, diagnosed, and/or medicated. This system of medicating does not allow for proper healing. Medication treats the behaviors and not the underlying causes. Here is a glimpse into signs and symptoms of the common disorders Anxiety, Depression, Post Traumatic Stress Disorder, Reactive Attachment Disorder, and Self-harm/Self-injury that plague foster youth.

Anxiety Disorder

Anxiety Disorder is an excessive fear or anxiety that is difficult to control and has a substantially negative impact on daily functioning. Fear refers to the emotional response to a real or perceived threat, while anxiety is the anticipation of a future threat. Symptoms may include:

- Panic attacks
- Avoidance of people, places, or conflict
- Periods of heart pounding, nausea, or dizziness
- Tendency to predict the worst
- Distress in social situations

Symptoms of Anxiety Disorder

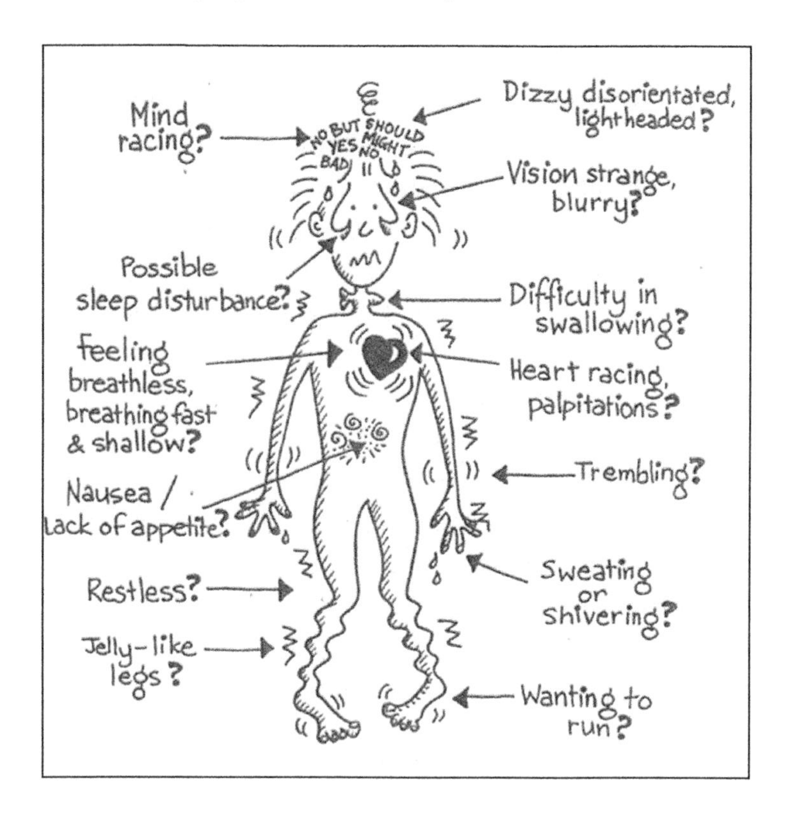

This may be the student who has an incessant need for details, so they ask a lot of questions or shy away from group activities. Anxiety and depression commonly co-occur.

Depression

Depression is a long-term melancholy mood that lasts for at least two weeks and affects a person's ability to go to work or school, or to carry out usual daily activities, or to engage in satisfying personal relationships.

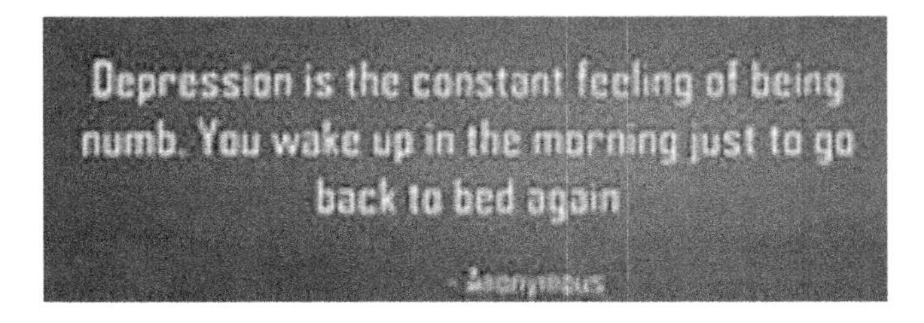

Symptoms may include:

- Moving more slowly or sometimes becoming agitated and unable to settle down
- Lack of energy or excessively tired
- Feeling worthless
- Thinking about death or dying
- Difficulty concentrating or making decisions

A student struggling with major depression may miss class or appointments with you or feel hopeless and say things like, "What's the point?"

PTSD – Post Traumatic Stress Disorder

Post Traumatic Stress Disorder (PTSD) is described as the development of debilitating symptoms following exposure to a traumatic or dangerous event. The intrusive symptoms may include:

- Flashbacks, upsetting dreams, or distressing memories
- Avoidance of stimuli associated with the traumatic event
- Changes in cognition and mood (e.g., dissociative amnesia, negative beliefs about oneself, and feelings of detachment or estrangement)
- Hyperarousal and hypervigilance, or exaggerated startle response
- Irritability or self-destructive behavior

Some causes of PTSD include:
Physical and sexual assault, occurring at the highest rate, sudden death of a loved one, transportation, illness/injury, accidents, and natural disasters. The following chart lists causes with a percentage representing frequency of occurrence.

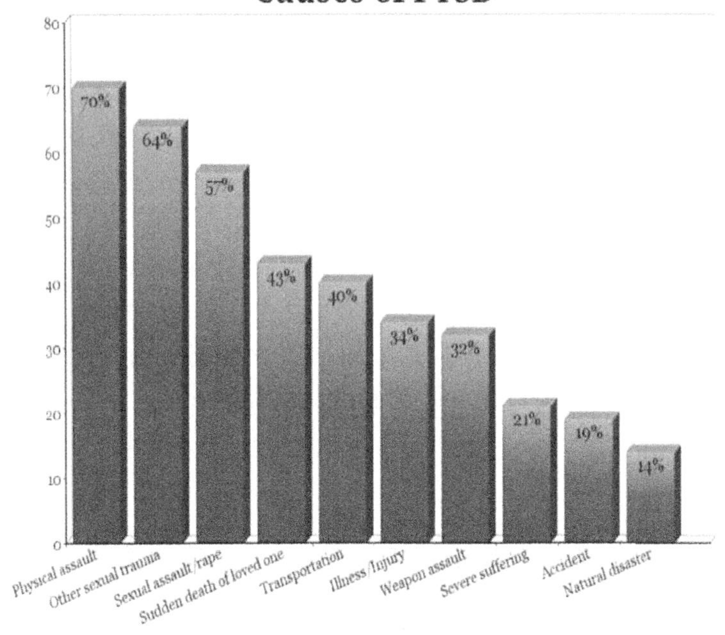

All youth in foster care suffer from Post Traumatic Stress Disorder (PTSD). If the only trauma a foster child ever experiences is being removed from their birth family, that is significant enough to have lasting effects. For most foster children, removal is not the first traumatic event nor is it the last. This removal perpetuates attachment issues.

RAD – Reactive Attachment Disorder

Reactive Attachment Disorder (RAD) is a severe consequence of a failed bond between a child and their primary caregiver. This basic loss ignites feelings of rejection and can result in ongoing feelings of rage, shame, lack of trust, a morbid fear of attaching to anyone, an inability to understand cause and effect thinking, and a compulsive need to control everyone and every situation. Manifestations of RAD include:

- Belief that relationships do not last and are contracts, which lead to thoughts of *What's in it for me?* or *People do not just care for "no reason."*
- Lying or stealing
- Intolerance for rules and restraints
- Altered sense of justice
- Suicide and self-harming are common • In adulthood, can become manipulative

For the young adult with RAD, trust does not come easy and manipulation is a way of life. They may negotiate to get exceptions to the rules even though they know the policies. We tell children to go to adults for assistance, but for foster youth who may have been taken from home after telling an adult, following the rules resulted in negative consequences. Based on these past experiences of following rules, rules seem unjust to a person with RAD.

Unfortunately, destructive behaviors, including self-harm, are symptoms of several of the disorders I have listed.

Self-Harm/Self-Injury

As a child, I had patches of hair missing from my eyelashes and eyebrows because I plucked them out. I wish someone had recognized that I was in distress and was engaging in self-harm. The specific manifestations of self-harm may vary from person to person. However, if you practice being empathetically trauma-informed, you will notice even small changes and prompt a conversation that shows you are concerned.

When someone intentionally causes harm to themselves in an impulsive and nonlethal way because they may feel lonely or empty inside, are over or under stimulated, or are unable to express their feelings, it is called self-harm. While it is not a specific mental illness, it is a symptom of mental distress.

Quiz: MYTHs vs FACTs about self-harm/self-injury

Statement	Myth or Fact
1. Only minors engage in self-harm.	
2. Self- harm is only physical.	
3. People self-harm to get attention.	
4. Self-injury is a failed suicide attempt.	

Answers:

1. **Myth** – anyone can self-harm
2. **Myth** - Forms of self-harm may include: excessive exercise, sabotaging relationships, staying in relationships with people who treat you badly, mixing medications with alcohol, and not seeking treatment when you are aware you have an illness.
3. **Fact and Myth** – People who self-harm are attention "needers." They may not have the words to communicate their needs and may feel they do not have anyone to confide in.
4. **Myth** – The intent is to harm oneself, not kill oneself.

Mental Health America reported that studies revealed college students engaged in self-injury at higher rates than adolescents (17-33% and 15%, respectively).

We have reviewed how trauma alters the brain's natural state of being, resulting in mental illness. Now, I would like to continue to look at connecting your knowledge of trauma by discussing potential impairment in long-term functioning and development. Specifically, some areas where you may see the greatest impact might include learning, social-emotional development, and adult outcomes.

Impaired Functioning

One of the long-term effects from living with trauma is impaired functioning. Students arrive on our campuses showing:

Learning

Trauma and stress overload the limbic system. The limbic system is the part of the brain responsible for affects/emotions, memory, sensory processing, time perception, attention, consciousness, instincts, autonomic/vegetative control, and actions/motor behavior. When this system is activated, the brain is in survival mode and other systems are less active. If your brain thinks the body is being chased by a two-ton bear, it is not open for things like learning new math concepts, new house/program rules, or even remembering all the elements of the Student Mutual Responsibility Contract.

When complex trauma occurs, the survival mode switch gets stuck in the "on" position and the other system switches are "off" or have limited functionality. When the limbic system is switched "on" and in charge, the following systems do not fully function:

- Temporal Lobes which are responsible for memory
- Occipital Lobes which oversee reading
- Basal Ganglia which house procedural learning

This limited functionality during "survival mode" makes it almost impossible to take in new information.

I recall one of my students, let's call her Jane, coming into the office exhibiting what I would describe as survival mode in action. She approached the worker at the counter rather aggressively and became angry because she needed a book voucher and was told there were none left. I happened to be in the office and overheard the encounter. I came out to greet Jane and asked her to come into my office to talk. Unfortunately, she was given incorrect information because she did not identify herself (nor was she asked) as a student in our cohort. Fortunately, the funding we receive allows me to provide vouchers even after the other programs run out.

When you have a distressed student at the counter who is upset, trying to reinforce office rules by telling them to keep their voice down will fall on deaf ears. The services and supports we provide to our students fulfill some basic survival needs—safety and psychological. When basic needs are threatened, our foster youth receive signals that trigger a familiar, yet uncomfortable sensation. The brain senses danger and reacts with fight, flight, or freeze. A student may become agitated and fight by arguing or yelling. One reaction to emotional distress is a heightening in the pitch of your voice. A person may not realize the change in their tone. Flight may look like them walking away from you in mid-sentence, usually muttering some colorful words. If the student seems to be stone-faced and not talking back to you while you are trying to explain what happened, this is a form of freezing. These negative interactions between students and staff because of program requirements can translate to an overall negative impression regarding school, ultimately affecting their academic performance. Programs could benefit students by addressing their social-emotional needs.

Suggested Trauma-Informed Response

Rather than addressing the specific behaviors, address the cause of distress. Firstly, do not have this conversation at the front counter, ask the student to step into a private office. Secondly, acknowledge the news may be disturbing and that you want to help. Finally, ask what happened that caused them to be out of compliance with program requirements.

One trauma-informed intervention might be to examine your program policies on how and when a student is notified about pending adverse program actions, such as disqualification. Our foster youth do experience some special circumstances around housing and stability that may affect their academic performance. Trust issues may interfere with students seeing program staff as a go-to source. While you may be aware of this, consider the ways you communicate to students and your openness to assist them before things hit critical mass. Clearly, articulating this openness can strengthen other areas, such as their social-emotional development, that could be reshaped from new positive relationships.

S T I R

Social-emotional Development

The National Child Trauma Stress Network does a great job illustrating the impact of trauma on social-emotional development. Below, Tables 2. 3, and 4, documents just a few of the developmental milestones by age. The second column provides a corresponding list of long-term effects when trauma happens and is untreated during the corresponding stage of development.

Table 2: Development Ages 0-5

Young Children (0-5)	
Key Developmental Tasks	**Impact From Trauma Exposure**
• Development of visual and auditory perception • Recognition of and response to emotional cues • Attachment to primary caregiver	• Avoidance of contact • Heightened startle response • Confusion about what is dangerous and who to go to for protection

Table 3: Development Ages 6-12

School Aged Children (6-12)	
Key Developmental Tasks	**Impact From Trauma Exposure**
• Manage fears, anxiety, and aggression • Sustain attention for learning and problem solving • Control impulses and manage physical responses to danger	• Emotional swings • Learning Problems • Specific anxieties and fears • Revert to younger behaviors

Table 4: Development Ages 13-21

Adolescence Children (13-21)	
Key Developmental Tasks	**Impact From Trauma Exposure**
• Think abstractly • Anticipate and consider the consequences of behavior and safety • Modify and control behavior to meet long-term goals	• Difficulty imagining or planning for the future • Over- or underestimating danger • Inappropriate aggression • Reckless and/or self-destructive behaviors

How can this information be useful? If a student has experienced complex trauma during these respective stages of development, a part of them is emotionally stagnant or stuck at that age. A person may age but not necessary develop the key skills that are supposed to be mastered at various stages of life. If you are fortunate enough to have knowledge of the age at which a student entered foster care, you may have a glimpse into where they may have socio-emotional development delays.

Adult Outcomes (ACEs Study)

We cannot talk about trauma without referencing the ACEs Study. "What is the ACEs study?" you ask. Let me share it with you. From 1995-1997, Kaiser conducted the Adverse Childhood Experiences Study (ACES) with 17,000 members responding to ten questions about their childhood experiences and current health status. A significant finding from this study showed there was a direct link between childhood trauma and adult onset of chronic disease, as well as depression, suicide, propensity for violence, and victimization from violence.

As the number of ACEs increased, there was an increase in the risk for additional types of trauma as well as health, social, and emotional problems. Higher ACEs scores are also associated with increased rates of absenteeism from work and serious issues with work performance. To further illuminate the long-term impact of trauma in childhood over the life span, let's look at the ACEs Pyramid in Figure 6. Here, we see that over a lifetime, exposure to ACEs impacts overall health and well-being.

Figure 6: ACES Impact Over A Lifetime

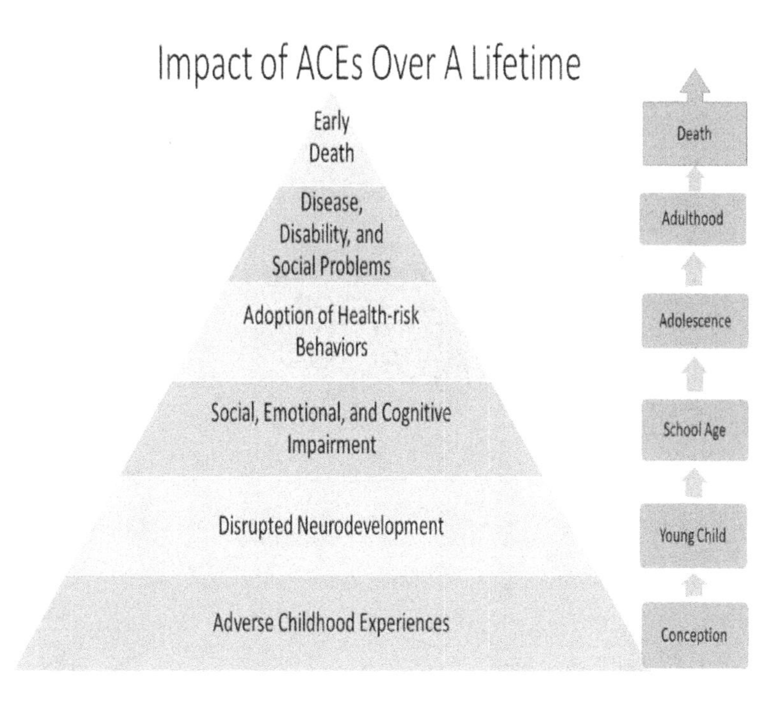

According to the pyramid, when trauma is experienced at a young age, resulting in a disruption in brain develop, there are lasting and even deadly consequences. Early intervention with children could improve their quality of life.

Applying It

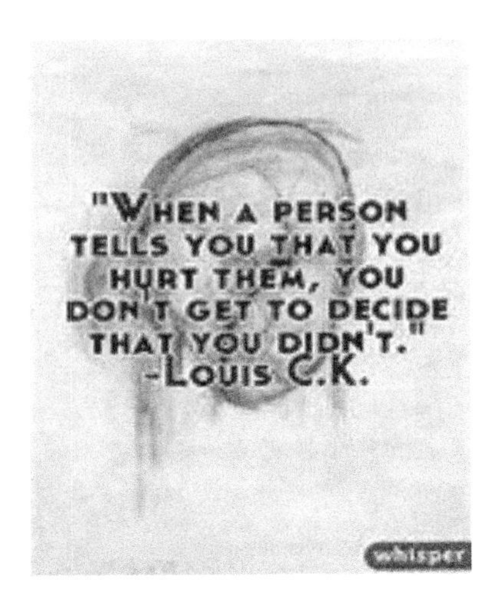

Thank you for letting me share parts of my story as we examine trauma. Now on to the fourth element for this chapter—Applying It. Here you will participate in an activity that will encourage you to reflect on the work we engaged in to define trauma and connect the definitions to long-term effects. In this Chapter 1 activity, Trauma Causes Wrinkles, you will hopefully tie it all together.

Activity: Trauma Causes Wrinkles

Materials: a small piece of paper and a pen.

Instructions:

1. Write the initials of a student you have worked with on the top right-hand corner of the paper.
2. Write a sentence telling what you know about the student's history or any "different" behaviors exhibited by the student
3. Crumple the paper into a ball (do not discard it).
4. Try to smooth out the paper so it lays flat on the table.

No matter how much you try, you cannot make the paper as flat as it was before you crumpled it. Even if you use an iron, it will always have some wrinkles.

Takeaway: Students who have experienced trauma will always have some "wrinkle" or reminder of the traumatic experience. While there are interventions that can help them "smooth out" the effects of trauma so they are not pervasive in their day-to-day lives, the trauma "wrinkle" could resurface. It may appear because of a trigger or reminder. A reminder could be a person, a sound, a smell, or a gesture.

What you can do to help: Help students recognize triggers so they can be more cognizant of when they happen, along with any antecedents that may show up in their body. Additionally, help them to be mindful of self-imposed situations that may trigger a relapse (i.e., birth family relationships, homelessness, not asking for help, or substance use issues).

2

Being Trauma Informed: Actions Speak Louder Than Words

Trauma-informed is the new buzz word. Even Oprah has joined the movement with an episode on 60 Minutes. There has been a lot of research providing insight into how childhood traumatic experiences might impact us into adulthood. I challenge you to take a personal call to action when working with students whom you know have experienced foster care or other potentially distressing events in childhood. This personal call to action may include reflecting on how your childhood experiences have shaped the person you are today.

My Story: I'm Fine

A few years ago, I was attending a Directors' Meeting for Foster/Kinship Care Education. It was there I was introduced to the trauma training produced by the National Child Traumatic Stress Network. The curriculum includes a twenty-two-minute video which is partially narrated by children to depict a child's perspective on foster care and adoption.

After I watched intently, in tears through the entire video, I had an awakening. I felt as if my story of beliefs and behaviors while in foster care was being laid out for everyone to see. So many things were explained, like why I plucked my eyelash and eyebrow hairs to the point of leaving bald spots. It illuminated conversations I had only engaged in with myself like, *What is wrong with me that my mother did not want me around?* or *If it hurts to pull my eyelashes out or I get embarrassed when people see the bald patches, why do I do it?* or *Why do I give up so easily on relationships?*

These were conversations the adults in my life should have initiated with me as I was exhibiting what I now know were signs of the effects of trauma. Because I wasn't defying adults, failing in school, or harming other children, everyone's belief was, "Oh, she's fine."

The truth is, I wasn't "fine." From that moment on, it became my mission to educate all whom I encountered about being trauma-informed, so that others are not being overlooked and dismissed as being "fine" and as a result, run the risk of being retraumatized by the very people who are intent on being helpful.

Defining It

For a person who experiences trauma, the residual effects of trauma on their feelings, thoughts, beliefs, and relationships (including their relationship with our Guardian Scholars-like programs) is considered "widespread impact." The widespread impact you see with the students you work with on a day-to-day basis can be overwhelming and have an impact on you as a professional. Utilizing this knowledge to provide more mental health and supportive services to foster youth on campus can aid in trauma recovery for both you and your students.

Trauma-Informed Principles

Let's look at the definition of trauma-informed from the Substance Abuse and Mental Health Services Administration (SAMHSA):

- Realizing the widespread impact of trauma and understanding potential paths for recovery.
- Recognizing signs and symptoms of trauma in clients, families, staff, and others involved with the system.

- Responding by fully integrating the knowledge about trauma into your policy, procedures, and practices.
- Seeking to actively resist re-traumatization.

These tenets provide a framework to consider for implementing trauma-informed engagement strategies. However, before you can practice, you must have a shift in your mind-set. It is not enough to learn the ways and then continue with business as usual if we are trying to affect a change in the outcomes for our students.

Shifting Your Mindset

We fear what we do not understand. So, understanding that people do not ask to be traumatized and cannot control the effects of it is the first step. While you may not ever know the extent of the person's trauma history, it is not an essential element in being empathetically trauma informed. I personally believe in the idea of TMI—too much information. I do not want to know every detail. I feel compelled to do something with information I learn, so I will only ask about what I need to know.

If you adopt a mind-set of being considerate of others' feelings and give credence to their pleas for understanding, you are beginning to shift your mindset. So, do not be afraid of the student who believes differently than you. Do not be afraid of the student with different childhood experiences from yours. Do not be afraid of the student who seems a little "quirky" or guarded or has trust issues.

It's Not Just a Clinical Term

While Trauma-Informed Care is a clinical term, it's not just looking at it from a clinical standpoint of, "Give me all the information I need to know." It is a choice to take in the information and have a different mind-set or perception about what you are seeing, how you respond to what you are seeing, and actually putting your response into practice. These actions should influence how you greet and treat students overall.

Would you put somebody behind the wheel and forcibly make them have a car accident? I would like to think not. The intent of being trauma-informed is to understand what has happened so we are not causing students to be traumatized every time they come to our offices, every time they come in for a counseling or advisement session, every time they come to pick up vouchers, or every time they come for workshops.

Being trauma-informed is about the way you respond, not react, to the things you see exhibited by the behaviors of your students. It also involves using the data available on student retention, persistence, and success rates to inform program decisions.

My Story: My Obsessive Behaviors

I have become the consummate "people-pleaser" and over achiever. As a child, I was the snitch. My mother had me convinced that she could tell when I was lying. She told me my hair would stand up. As a child, I believed her. In retrospect, I know that wasn't really possible. I have never shaved my legs—I do not grow that much hair—and I had even less hair as a child. That fable was among a few ways I lived with emotional abuse as a child.

My siblings did not like for "the little sister" to tag along when they played with their friends, especially if they were planning to be mischievous. I would tell them, "Why would you do that when you know you are going to get in trouble with Mom?" My brother told me, "Yeah, we get in trouble because you tell." As adults, we talked about how that affected our sibling relationships. As a child, I suffered from isolation. What my siblings did not know was the torment I experienced by either being bribed or my mother threatening to whip me, so I would tell her what happened.

This began my cycle of trying to be good to avoid the physical abuse I witnessed inflicted on my siblings. I was the good student who did not get calls home from school. I was the good daughter, doing my chores and running to my mother's beckoning call so I wouldn't get punished. I created copious to-do lists and lofty goals so I could prove that I was good enough (I still engage in these obsessive behaviors). My efforts proved to not be good enough to keep my mother from putting me into foster care. This led to my feelings of rejection and abandonment which still surface to this day.

I carried these behaviors into adulthood trying to be the agreeable girlfriend and wife (two times). I performed in this role until it felt uncomfortable or no longer worked in my favor. So, I would abandon the relationship—I'm going to reject you before you reject me.

My obsessive-compulsive behaviors still persist. I am still known for juggling multiple major life projects at once. As I am penning this book, I'm enrolling in a doctoral program, securing funding to continue providing Mental Health First Aid trainings, contracting as a consultant under four different contracts, working a full-time job at the college. and teaching a part-time assignment. Yes, most of this is to make sure the bills are paid. Another part stems from a foster youth belief about psychological safety and reverting to survival mode to never be without. Finally, the need for multiple streams of income prevents me from depending on others and possibly encountering rejection—again. This obsessive behavior is a vicious cycle. It is exhausting, frustrating, and overwhelming and causes me to shut down, then get frustrated for taking on so much, and triggering self-doubting beliefs about my abilities. I know I have limits. However, eventually my compulsive need to complete my to-do list is triggered and I dive back into my work pattern. So, why do I continue in this cycle of behavior?

Connecting It

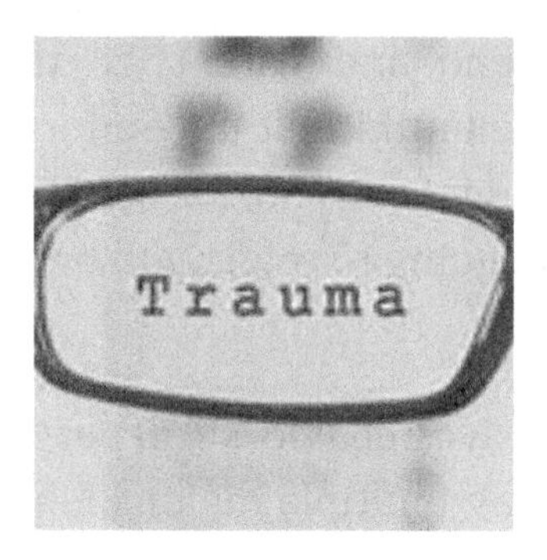

We often judge a person on the surface by their behaviors. A part of being trauma-informed is to consider the reasons for, and the feelings behind, what is exhibited, in order to try and understand the behavior. I call this viewing people through a trauma lens.

Behaviors, Reasons, and Feelings

Being a people-pleaser and an over-achiever are just two scenarios of behaviors I carry into adulthood that are manifestations of things I experienced in childhood. These behaviors are connected to reasons and feelings. The Cognitive Behavioral Triangle illustrates the connectivity of behaviors to reasons and feelings.

Scenario #1:

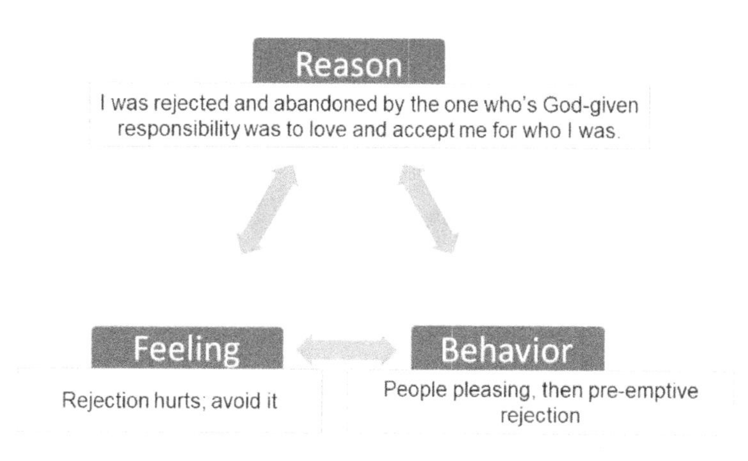

In Scenario One, the "People-pleaser":

- **Behavior** – People pleasing and preemptive rejection
- **Feeling** –Rejection hurts; so avoid being rejected
- **Reasoning/Thought** – I was rejected and abandoned by the one whose God-given responsibility was to love and accept me for who I was. When things got uncomfortable

  for my mother because of the changes I was going through due to my developmental stage, she rejected me. I later came to learn that my mother was repeating a cycle. At age thirteen, she too was sent away by her mother. This developmental milestone was a trigger for her.

Scenario #2:

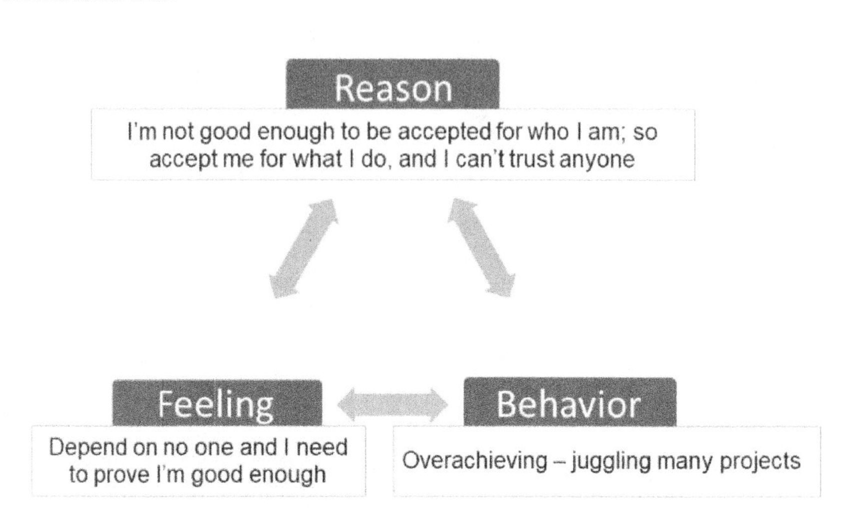

In scenario two, the "Over Achiever":

- **Behavior** – overachieving by creating extensive to-do lists with lofty goals and juggling multiple projects.
- **Feeling** – I plan so I am never without basic necessities or wants and never depend on someone else. Also, I need to prove I'm good enough.
- **Reasoning/Thought** – I want to be accepted. I'm not good enough to be accepted for who I am. So, I seek acceptance for what I do or to avoid loneliness. Also, I cannot trust anyone to take care of me because people are not true to their word.

Our role as student services professionals affords us to see a variety of students and many varying behaviors. When we see behaviors in others that we do not understand or do not like, we just want them to stop. This reaction comes from our own place of discomfort and lack of knowledge. As you seek to be empathetically trauma-informed, it will be helpful to keep in mind the elements of the Cognitive Behavioral Triangle. Using the triangle does not mean you have to know exactly what a student is feeling or the reasons behind the feeling. You can ask if you really need to know.

Suggested Trauma-Informed Response

Being empathetically trauma-informed is more about being aware of, and sensitive to, the possible layering of feelings and reasons for unusual behavior and not just taking a behavior at face value. Rather than being annoyed with a student's particular action, ask yourself what might that student be feeling in the moment and why might they be feeling this way? How do you feel when someone is not understanding of your behaviors? We all have some behaviors or quirks that are not readily understood by others.

S
T
I
R

The "What's Wrong Tango"

You: "Hi friend; what's wrong?" Friend: "Nothing."

You: "No, really, what's wrong with you?"

Friend: "Nothing."

You: "I know something is wrong with you, so what is it?"

Friend: "Nothing." You: "Alright, see you later."

Friend: (angrily says) "You always do this; you do not really care. You just gonna walk away?"

You: "What? I asked you what was wrong with you."

This is a human dance in which we have all participated. It starts with bantering back and forth, then leads to an argument about everything but the real issue. Now there are hurt feelings on both sides and no resolution. Interestingly, when the tables are turned and a friend asks you, "What's wrong?", the dance is performed yet again.

So, what is the problem with engaging in the *What's Wrong Tango*? The problem is, we are asking the wrong question, so it is not yielding the desired results. No one wants to feel like something is wrong with them, that they aren't accepted, or that they do not belong. Now you ask me, "How can I avoid getting entangled in the unhealthy human relationship *What's Wrong Tango?"*

Good question. You can try saying something like this instead:

> You: "I am concerned about you because I see...; is there something you would like to talk about?"

State what you observe is different—not "wrong" from their usual way of being, e.g., they are not smiling, their hair isn't combed, or they are not responding to calls or text messages. By addressing the situation from a place of concern, you demonstrate that you are very aware of the person's existence and that you value them. If you do this, they will be less likely to feel defensive and more apt to respond positively.

What are some of your quirks or things people notice that you do differently? We all have something. Do you squeeze the toothpaste from the bottom or the middle of the tube? Do you like to plan all the details of the friends' outings so you know everything will be taken care of? Do you arrive everywhere fifteen minutes early? Are you the one everybody tells to arrive fifteen minutes ahead of the real time because you are always late? Do you have an undying passion for orderliness? Do you have a hard time staying focused in a meeting? Are you shy? Do you point out what could go wrong in any situation? Do you engage in "retail therapy"? Do you struggle with indecisiveness?

How do you feel when someone calls you on your quirks or proclaims you are doing something the wrong way because your way is different from theirs? All of the aforementioned quirks, in excess, could be signs of a mental disorder. Working from a trauma-informed mind-set, we recognize that we all have a little something "different" going on. Just as you want to be understood and accepted, those who have extreme "quirks" because of traumatic experiences, want and deserve to be understood and accepted. Practicing trauma-informed engagement can reduce the potential of re-traumatizing the very person you are trying to help.

Avoid Re-Traumatization

SAMHSA reminds us to "actively resist retraumatization". Have you encountered someone who was nosy and asked you intrusive questions? I believe there really are dumb questions when it comes to engaging with someone who has experienced trauma. A dumb question is one that is asked unnecessarily, that could have harmful repercussions, and could be potentially traumatizing.

One practice I have to minimize re-traumatization is not asking about family members or past intimate partners when I encounter someone I have not seen for a long time. I have a fear that if they have experienced a traumatic event associated with the person that I have asked about, my asking may trigger them and cause them to break out in tears or have some other negative reaction akin to symptoms of PTSD. I do not want to carry that kind of burden; I already have too much emotional baggage of my own.

Oprah Winfrey did a segment for 60 Minutes on trauma-informed care. I applaud her for delving into her own childhood experiences to bring awareness to this issue. The show also featured known Psychologist, Dr. Bruce Perry. I agree with Dr. Perry's statement, "Relationships make the difference in recovery from the effects of trauma." However, I disagree with the strategy offered by Oprah to ask, "What happened to you?" This question can be re-traumatizing and the honest answer may be, "I do not know." Why do you really want to know what happened? Later in the book, I will share some insights into the types of experiences of children who are, or were, in foster care as a backdrop to what possibly happened.

Recounting distressing past events can be retraumatizing. It is possible that a person may not know what happened. Unfortunately, for some, they get stuck in survival mode. The brain may have repressed the memories or disassociated from the event itself. Both are strategies the brain uses to switch into survival mode.

Repressed memories – Webster's defines repressed as, "Stopped from being expressed or remembered." Repression of memories that are too difficult or unacceptable to deal with is an automated process to exclude them from our consciousness. This differs from suppression in that suppression is a conscious process.

Disassociation – avoiding conscious awareness of a traumatic event while it is occurring or for an indefinite time following.

> *"I do not think there was a time when I wasn't abused as a child. In order to survive the abuse, I made myself believe that the real me was separated from my body. That way, the abuse*

was happening not really to me, but just to this skin I'm in." - C. M

Do Not Ask What Happened

I feel the strategy offered to ask someone who has experienced trauma, "What happened to you?" goes against trauma-informed principles because it can be re-traumatizing. Being empathetically trauma-informed means, you now have an awareness that trauma and its effects are widespread.

I would like to reiterate the definition of empathy: *the action of understanding, being aware of, being sensitive to, and vicariously experiencing the feelings, thoughts, and experiences of another, of either the past or present, without having the feeling, thoughts, and experience fully communicated in an objectively explicit manner.*

So, knowing the details of what happened to a person is not a requirement in practicing trauma-informed engagement.

Do Not Ask Me Why I Did That

If you ask a child, "Why did you do that?" The answer will likely be "I do not know."

If I ask you, "Why do you continue to smoke when you know it's not healthy for you?" or, "Why do you continue to drive faster than 65 MPH on the freeway when you know you could get a ticket?" or, "Why do you yell (walk away, shut down, drink, etc.,) when you get angry?" or,

"Why do you have a hard time spelling?" Your answer is likely to be, "I do not know."

Suggested Trauma-Informed Response

If you witness a student exhibiting a troubling behavior, try asking, "What sensation were you feeling in your body just before you did... or said...?" The key is to help students recognize the sensations in their body that the brain is giving as a signal. Something the student experienced (i.e., disagreement with a teacher or a request for assistance being ignored, or someone violating their space) is triggering the limbic system to go into survival mode. This results in a fight (arguing), flight (walking out of class) or freeze (not answering your question or saying, "I do not know" or, "I do not want to talk about it") response.

S T I R

Helping students to understand what is going on in their body as a response to an emotion, can help them to identify triggers and find new ways to address, and even change, their reactions.

Applying It

Putting It Into Practice

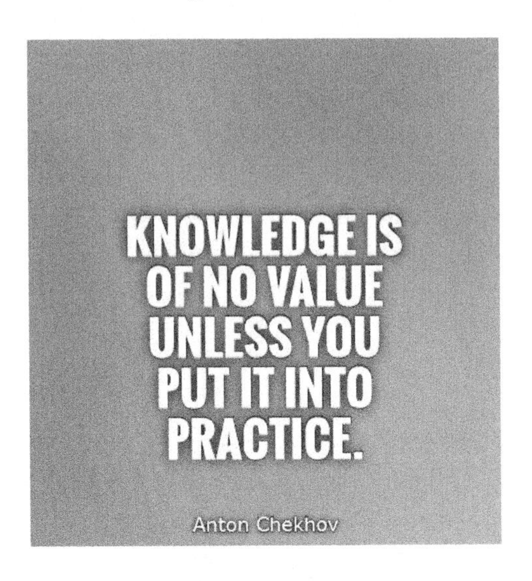

Communities that provide a context of understanding and self-determination may facilitate the healing and recovery process for the individual. Alternatively, communities that avoid, overlook, or misunderstand the impact of trauma may often be re-traumatizing and interfere with the healing process. Individuals can be re-traumatized by the very people whose intent is to be helpful.
~SAMSHA

Activity: Heart, Mind and Feet

Now that you have some information on being empathetically trauma-informed, let's look at how you will use this knowledge personally and in your program:

1. Some things I will take to heart:

____
____
____

2. Some things I will bear in mind:

____
____
____

3. Some things I will put feet to (take action):

____
____
____

4. Some program changes that can be made immediately that will demonstrate trauma-informed principles (e.g., greeting and interacting with students, our forms, contracts, and program participation requirements):

____
____
____

3

The Connection Between Foster Care and Trauma

Can you recall your first date, first kiss, first car accident, or the first day of school? These are all memorable occasions. If you ask any person who has been in foster care, they will be able to recall, in great detail, the events of the first day they went into foster care. It is not something easily forgotten. My story is not drastically different from many other youths'.

My Story: My First Placement

For a thirteen-year-old nerd from Pasadena, living in South Central Los Angeles was like going to a foreign country. As Barbara, the social worker drove, I tried to pay attention to how we got to the house just in case I needed to make a quick escape. The only thing I remembered was the Thrifty drugstore on Vermont.

Thrifty's became my place of solace that summer. To get out of the house, I would walk five blocks to get an ice cream cone with the change I had been given by my sister. She would give change to me when she would return to the house after staying out all night or several nights.

After passing Thrifty's, we arrived at a corner house on Eighty something and Budlong. The house looked small and scary. I had never visited, let alone lived in, a house with security bars on the windows. Barbara, knocked on the door and "Madame T" greeted us. "Madame T" is the name I gave that foster mom once I became an adult after finding out some of the awful things she orchestrated. She was an older lady, probably only in her 50s but to a thirteen-year-old, that's old. She smiled and seemed friendly enough, but I could not then and still cannot imagine calling her "mom," like many children in foster care are forced to do.

There were three bedrooms for six girls. Today, this setting is known as a small family home—not a family foster home nor a group home. This is usually the type of placement for children with higher levels of misbehavior. My sister and I arrived to fill beds four and five. Since my sister was sixteen and I was thirteen, we had to sleep in different rooms. I was not happy with these sleeping arrangements.

My record player and I set up shop in the bed closest to the door, thinking it was the shortest escape route. I never owned very many clothes since I was a size zero, which was not a very popular size at the time. I was also at the awkward stage of development where I was too tall for girl's clothing but not mature enough for women's clothes. Most pants were too short so I had one pair of red women's slacks, four "Little House on the Prairie" dresses, and a pair of roller coaster shoes from Thom McCann—what a sight. A few days later, Madame T took me shopping at her friend's boutique where she bought me silky panties and a t-shirt with a roller skate on the front.

When we met the other girls, it was akin to introducing a new fish into a tank. The old fish test the newbies to establish dominance. The other girls eyeballed us from head to toe, snarling with indifference and hovering around their sleeping areas as if to mark their territory—what a warm welcome! Dinnertime was an interrogation session where the others tried to feel out the new kids. Eventually, the tensions subsided and the girls realized I was harmless, but the verdict was still out on my sister. For anyone entering a new domicile, this initial pressure can be crippling.

I kept to myself most of the time. If you asked the other girls, they might say I was shy. However, if you have met or heard of me, you would know "shy" is not an adjective that describes me. No, I wasn't shy. I was living in a strange house with people I didn't know, and I did not know why. I was scared, withdrawn, lonely, grief-stricken, and confused. I just wanted to be home with my mommy and siblings.

I went to bed that night but cannot say I slept. I wanted to sleep in hopes that my mother would shake me to awaken me from this lonely nightmare. Instead, it was Madame T's house assistant telling me to get dressed because it was time for breakfast. I thought, *Dang! I'm still here!*

Defining It

In my dictionary, you will see trauma listed as a synonym for foster care. Each time a child is taken from their home and forced to live somewhere else, no matter the reason and even if it is a better situation, the experience is traumatic. For those who work with foster youth, being educated on trauma and trauma-informed principles is only part of the solution. Children who are a part of the child welfare system need special considerations. Many of the strategies presented for helping someone heal from exposure to trauma, are not applicable to foster youth. One such strategy is to have consistent adult support. Given that within the first eighteen months in foster care, a child moves an average of four times and older youth live in an average of ten different homes, the system nullifies the possibility of consistency. This note is from my dictionary and first-hand knowledge. Chapter three gives empirical evidence to provide a portrait of the foster care system.

What Is Foster Care?

So, what is foster care you ask? Good question. It is a system designed to provide a temporary home for children whose parents are unable to take care of them. Children who are in foster care become wards of the court or wards of the state. So, our father is the governor. Today, in 2018, that would make us "Jerry's kids". Funny, he was governor when I first went into care.

We aren't going to delve into the complicated questions about ward of court status or age of eligibility. I will have a page that references the giant two-inch manuals which provide that detailed information. Alternately, you can invite me for a consult to address these questions.

How Children Enter Foster Care

Children enter foster care because someone reported suspected abuse or neglect. An investigation is completed to determine whether the allegation is legitimate or false. If it proves to be true, then the claim of abuse or neglect is "substantiated." In other words, there is significant evidence that the child is suffering from abuse or neglect.

Figure 7 shows statistics from 2015. There were almost 500,000 calls to the Child Abuse Hotline alleging abuse or neglect. After investigating the calls, about 69,000 were proven to show verifiable evidence of maltreatment. However, of these 69,000 cases, only approximately 27,000 resulted in children being removed from their homes. "Why did they not remove all 69,000?" you ask. There are several possible reasons for the vast difference in the numbers:

1. The non-custodial parent was located, so the child went to live with them.
2. Another relative stepped up to take the children.
3. Supports were provided in-home to help reduce further risk.

Figure 7: 2015 Foster Care Statistics

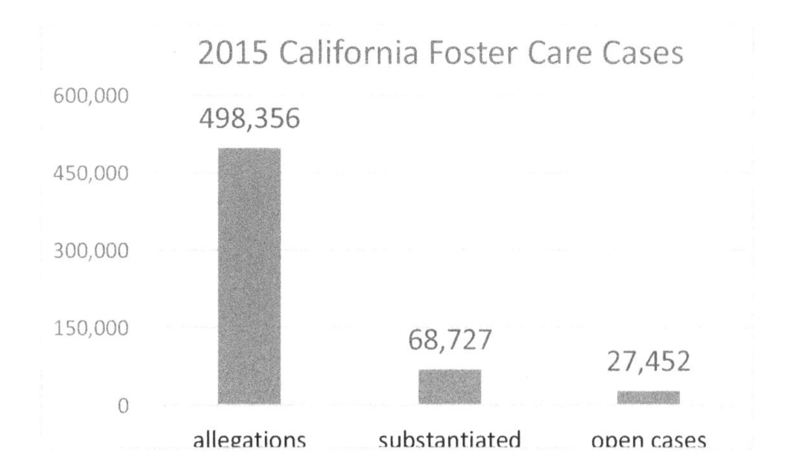

For those allegations that resulted in the opening of a foster care case, the child could be sent to a number of different living situations or placements.

Types of Placements

Foster care is intended to provide temporary, safe living arrangements and therapeutic services for children who cannot remain safely at home due to child maltreatment or for children whose parents are unable to provide adequate care.

Figure 8: 2016 California Foster Care Placements By Type

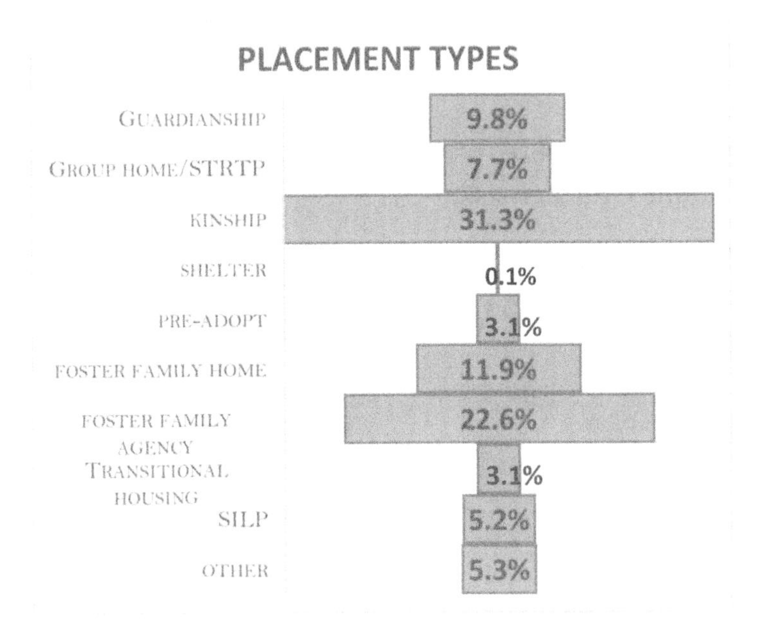

Looking at the statewide data in Figure 8, about 31% of foster youth are placed with relatives in **kinship** care (in Los Angeles County it's over 50%). Besides blood relatives such as grandparents, siblings, and aunt/uncles, caregivers in this category can also be classified as non-related extended family members (NREFM). NRFEMs are adults who have had a previous familiar relationship with the child such as a teacher, coach, or god parent.

Foster family homes and **foster family agencies** account for a combined total of approximately 35%

of placements. Foster family agencies are still foster homes. Private agency social workers serve as an intermediary between the caregivers and the department of children and family services. This usually provides a cushion and additional support to the caregivers.

Guardianship or legal guardianship is court approved custody through either the Juvenile Dependency or Probate Court. Close to 10% of youth are placed in this category. Guardianship is a permanency option that may be preferable over adoption (especially with relatives.) It allows for the guardian to make all legal decisions for the child without interference from the birth parent.

Group home is a residential treatment facility for children who need a high level of therapeutic care to help them manage behaviors or transition back into a stable home environment. As of January 2017, the law requires group homes to recertify under more stringent regulations as a Short-Term Residential Therapeutic Program (STRTP), to provide more intensive supports in a shortened timeframe. Statewide, approximately 10% of foster youth live in this type of placement.

Once a youth turns eighteen, they have the option of keeping their foster care case open until the age of twenty-one. This extension provides for the placement option of **transitional housing** (THP) (3.1%) or **Supervised Independent Living Program** (SILP) (5.2%). In either of these situations, a young person can live on their own. Through THP,

youth usually live in a shared apartment and are assigned a case manager to assist with life skills. Students placed in SILP may rent their own apartment or room or live in the college dorm.
The placement category of "other" represents about 5.3% of all placements. This category could include:

- Emergency shelter care, which is designed to house children for seventy-two hours up to two weeks
- Home of parent/voluntary placement where the child was not specifically removed but the parent is being monitored by the courts
- Runaways
- Home of parent (HOP aka voluntary placement). For this type of placement, the child was not removed from the home. However, in an effort to preserve the family unit, the parent volunteers to meet requirements established by DCFS (such as counseling or parenting classes). Failure to do so will result in the child being removed and a foster care case opened.

The category of HOP is one you may encounter when having challenges with obtaining a ward of court verification. Unfortunately, some students are not aware that they were never actually in foster care. They had a social worker to constantly monitor the family. They have the pains of removal and may have greater traumatic effects because they remained in the home where some level of maltreatment was still occurring, and no required mental health supports were being provided.

Voluntary placement has a different meaning today than it did back in the 80s. I was put into foster care because my mother "voluntarily put me in placement." The foster care system is grossly overloaded, so that is really no longer an option. Today, voluntary placement (or home of parent) means DCFS will monitor the family and if the parent does not voluntarily adhere to the requirements imposed by DCFS and the courts (i.e., parenting classes, removal of the offending adult, or drug testing), then the child(ren) will be removed and a foster care case opened.

Types of Abuse/Neglect

Maltreatment of children can come in many forms. I am not going to get into any graphic detail in connecting the types of abuse, but I will highlight a few distinguishing factors. Figure 9 shows the percentage of children who enter foster care based on the types of substantiated abuse.

Figure 9: Types Of Abuse

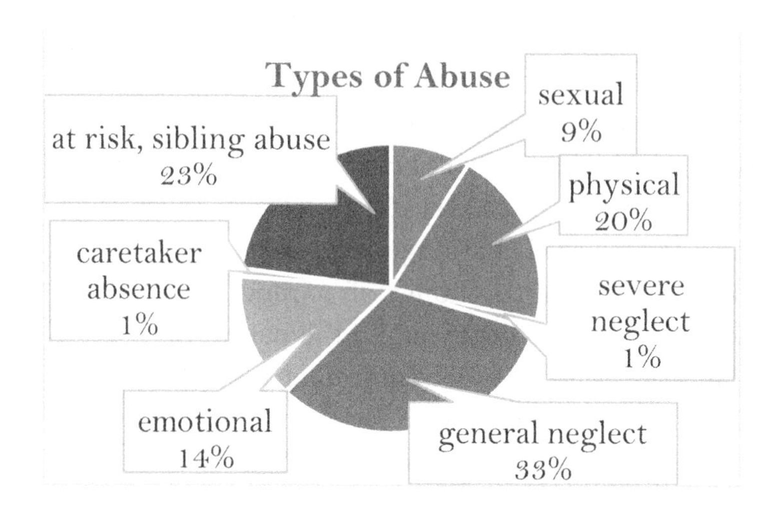

Neglect represents the highest rate of abuse at 34% combined (general neglect 33% and severe neglect, 1%). Children's Bureau defines neglect as:

> The failure of a parent or other person with responsibility for the child to provide needed food, clothing, shelter, medical care, or supervision to the degree that the child's health, safety, and well-being are threatened with harm.

There is a high percentage (23%) of children "at risk" for abuse because it has been substantiated that a sibling has been abused and possibly already removed from the home. Therefore, a child remaining in the home is also at risk of maltreatment.

Sexual abuse cases, reported at 9%, also include those who have been rescued from Commercial

Sexual Exploitation. This is a growing horrific crime that disproportionately targets foster youth as victims.

The approximately 1% of cases where there is an absence of a primary caregiver could include the incapacitation due to health and mental health issues or incarceration. No matter the circumstances behind the maltreatment, the separation that occurs has a significant and wide-spread impact.

Effects of Separation

Separation can be hugely traumatizing. Have you ever gotten separated from your parent in the store, or have you ever been the parent who lost your child in the store for a brief time? No matter which side of that scenario you were on, it seemed like an eternity before you were able to either reconnect. If you ask a child how long they were away from their parent they might say, "Forever." It was probably only about ten to twenty minutes. Separation is a type of loss that can lead to feelings of rejection and abandonment.

I recall a conversation with a colleague who had been removed from her father's care because of suspected abuse at the age of six. The two weeks that she was away from her custodial parent and temporarily placed in a foster home were very traumatizing, and she said, "It seemed like forever." As she spoke, her eyes glazed over, on the verge of tears. To this day, it is still painful for her to think about that short period away from her family. I know that pain all too well.

My Story: Waiting For The Visit

It is not unusual for teens to get excited about spending time with everyone other than their parents. This isn't necessarily the reality for children in foster care.

It seemed like a lifetime since I had seen my mother, two brothers, and two sisters, who were still living with my mother. The school week had come and gone. I guess I went since I had to be severely ill and have a note from the doctor to allow me to miss a day of school. TGIF had a whole new meaning—it meant Saturday was next and my mother was coming to visit. My mother was the best cook ever. She had promised to cook for me and bring dinner so I could share it with my new family.

Normally, I would do my chores on Saturday, but, since my mom was coming, I did them early. Saturday finally arrived! I was up early, annoying everyone else with my jittery excitement. The clock seemed to be moving in slow motion. Noon came and went, one o'clock came and went, and two o'clock came and went. By five o'clock, I knew she wasn't coming. I felt such a heavy burden of abandonment. This type of abandonment can trigger the grief and loss cycle.

Grief and Loss

Whenever a person experiences a loss, they must go through the grieving process. It is an automated process essential to human survival. Loss of connectedness to a parent is a real loss. Figure 10 illustrates the process of grieving.

Figure 10: Grief and Loss Cycle

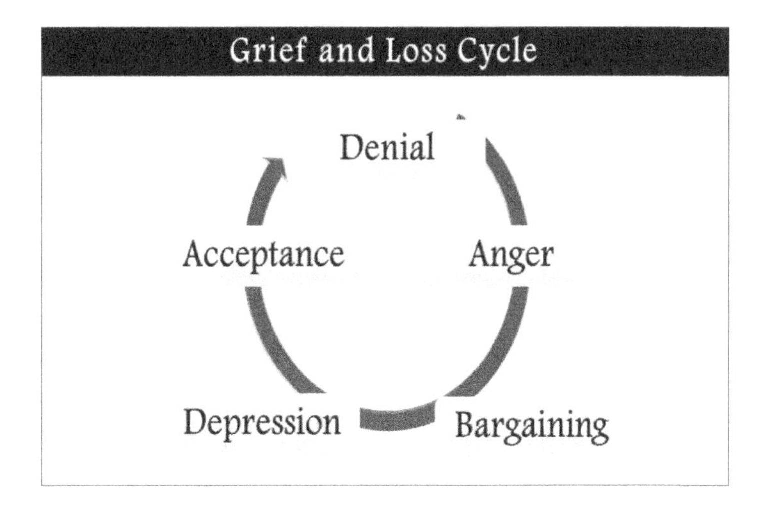

There is no set time for how long it will take a person to complete the cycle, nor how long they may languish in each stage. The only certainty is that the cycle must be completed. You can help by encouraging a person who is grieving to allow the feelings to flow and to seek counsel when they feel overwhelmed, stuck, or out of control.

Foster youth experience many losses:

- birth family
- siblings
- favorite toys
- innocence
- trust
- control

With each loss, children in foster care go through the grief and loss cycle—even multiple losses simultaneously, each with their own cycle to complete. Sometimes, the process is halted due to other survival events taking precedence. Even if the process is interrupted, at some point it must and will resume. As students get comfortable in the college environment, they may resume the cycle and not know it.

Rather than go through the pain again, children in foster care feel it is better to not get attached to anything or anyone. In one of our weekly Dine and Discover sessions, I had a student tell me, "You know we do not like to talk to others and it is difficult to make friends, or connections and..." She stopped in mid-sentence and said, "Oh, that is why you have us come here, huh?" I laughed as she had the revelation that I am aware of the losses and lack of trust developed in foster youth and want to help foster a sense of community. That investment in trust and community building paid off. I recently received a graduation announcement from her!

Rejection/Abandonment

Many foster youth harbor a great deal of guilt because of the separation from their birth family. For some, the loss of sibling connection is of greater consequence than parental loss. While children in foster care are painfully aware of the maltreatment inflicted on them by a parent, the reasons why can never be fully explained. Yes, I now know that my mother experienced a traumatic event at age thirteen at the hand of her mother. However, it doesn't help me to understand why my mother rejected me by placing me into foster care or abandoning me by not showing up for visits. I did not do anything wrong to her.

That sinking feeling of being abandoned is an emotional response that activates pain responses in the brain because our basic survival is threatened. There is no recovery from or explanation for the threat, so the system remains engaged for an extended, unhealthy period of time. This extension causes the brain to form new patterns to avoid reexperiencing the sensation because our thoughts, feelings, and behaviors are damaged when we experience rejections. Our primal brain recalls what it was like to be rejected from our tribe. It was analogous to being sentenced to death. Without inclusion by the group, it is nearly impossible to survive when basic needs such as access to shelter, food, protection, and the ability to procreate are unmet.

Dr. Guy Winch is a noted Psychologist who writes and speaks about emotional first aid. He shares an enlightening study conducted in a waiting room on the effects of rejection by strangers. In the study, the test subject believes they are waiting to be called in to participate in a study, not realizing the experiment had already begun in the waiting room. Originally, the test subject was included in a game of toss the ball. After a few rounds, the other players stopped throwing the ball to the test subject yet continued playing the game. Most people will say, "It would not have bothered me; they were strangers, so it would be no big deal that they stopped engaging." However, Dr. Winch explains that the emotional pain following rejection:

> *"...affects our thinking, floods us with anger, erodes our confidence and self-esteem, and destabilizes our fundamental feeling of belonging."* – Dr. Winch

Brain images of test subjects following these experiments showed activation of the same area of the brain where physical pain is registered. That is powerful pain! This pain from exclusion and separation can be exacerbated by birth family issues.

Birth Family Issues

> *"You do not choose your family. They are God's gift to you, as you are to them."* - Desmond Tutu

For foster youth, our lives are filled with sordid stories of family dynamics and may not feel like there is a "gift" exchange. Birth family dynamics can be so convoluted for foster youth. Here are a few scenarios that can be troublesome:

- Sometimes, the birth family involvement can be disruptive to the placement. For a child, visitations can take them on an emotional roller coaster. While they may want to see their family, it is an adjustment preparing for the visit, then readjusting back to the routine of the foster home. There are cases where the birth parent disrupts the household by making accusations, unscheduled visits and phone calls, or missing visits.

- Adding to the emotional roller coaster may be questions around why the youth is the only one of the children in foster care while the siblings remain home with the parent or were not abused.

- Siblings or other family members may blame the child for "telling" and separating the family or causing an investigation where secrets about the family tree are revealed. This may lead to siblings being separated because it is discovered they have different fathers.

- A child may have divided loyalties between the foster parent and birth parent. Birth parent(s) have been known to undermine the placement by telling the child not to obey or like the foster parent. Conversely, a foster parent may sabotage the family reunification because they disapprove of the birth parent and feel they are providing a better home for the child.

- I have students who have become the caretaker for the parent who was unable to take care of them.

I had a 19-year old student worker; we shall call him Joe. Joe's mother was in a sober living program and continuously would violate the program contract. The agency told Joe that if he did not attend family therapy sessions to get his mother to comply, they would dismiss her from the program and send her to live with him. We worked to adjust his schedule so he could participate.

Some of the circumstances around family issues can be emotionally draining or traumatizing. Sadly, I have heard many heart-wrenching stories. I would like to share two stories of my birth family issues.

My Story: Dear Mama

It took some years for me to get to a place of forgiveness with my mother for rejecting and abandoning me. How could she send me away? I was a good kid. I slept with her at night just in case she had an epileptic seizure. I stayed home from school, so she wasn't alone, especially after the many hospitalizations because of her Sickle Cell Anemia and Epilepsy. I ratted out my siblings as she requested. I did not get in trouble at school. What else was I supposed to do?

Years later, I came to realize that it was not me. There was no list of tasks I could have performed nor behaviors I could have corrected that would have changed my fate. A couple who knew my mother and her history from Louisiana enlightened me regarding my mother's childhood experiences. When my mother was thirteen, she was chased away at gunpoint by her mother. Subsequently, that trauma programmed her brain to think that children are no longer to be dealt with after the age of thirteen. As we all reached the age of thirteen, we were sent away. My oldest brother went into foster care. My older sister was sent to live with our biological grandfather, and I went into foster care.

My Story: Who's Your Daddy?

Months before my mother died, she again asked me, "If I could find your dad, would you like me to?" Even at age twenty-five, I was still curious about the person who gave me the other half of my DNA. I did not want anything from him. I did not secretly long for him to be a millionaire and advance me my inheritance. I wasn't even mad that he wasn't in my life. Out of all my mother's eleven children, only the last five experienced having their father in the house with them. So, it wasn't that I was jealous or wished he would come back, there was simply a knowledge void in me that I wanted to fill. I had no idea how deep this void would become.

Throughout my life, I had "daddy issues." Some say I like to date older men because I was looking for a father figure. I can neither confirm nor deny this theory. Growing up, my mother's stepfather was incredibly involved in our lives. I thought it was cool that "granddad" was there for our family. I recall, as a child, getting together with extended family at church because he was also our pastor. Exact relationships are not clearly defined. To me, all the children were cousins. It wasn't until after my mother passed that I got a better understanding of who these family members were.

Ten years after my mother's death, I reconnected with my mother's stepsister. During a visit, "my aunt" asked me, "Do you know who your sister's father is?" The question caught me off-guard. Throughout my childhood, there were rumors about our fathers, but the subject was taboo. So, I replied, "Oh, I don't really know." She proceeded to tell me that the man we called granddad was really my sister's father. I thought, *"Oh, okay."* Then she dropped the bomb, “He is also your father.” I immediately stood up and said, “I am leaving!”

Two months later at his funeral, the topic resurfaced. As I was standing next to his open casket, I saw him in a way I had never experienced before. It wasn’t as if I was seeing him for the first time, but it was like I was looking into a sick, twisted mirror. As I stood paralyzed with disbelief, I recognized my older brother and sister in his features. I viewed the adjacent picture and felt such a coldness, as if the blood was being sucked from my body. I realized, for the first time, that I had his eyes. I began to panic internally and longed for my sister to walk through the door to rescue me from this nightmare.

I carried around a lot of anger after this revelation. I was angry at him. I thought, “We should never have been put into foster care when our father was around the whole time.” I was angry at my mother for not telling me and pretending someone else was my father. I was angry at my newly discovered sisters. I was angry at one for being so cold and messy with the way she revealed the family secret, and I was angry at the other for being around me for years, even while I was in foster care, and not telling me the truth. We had even crossed paths in our professional lives, yet she had never sat me down to gently tell me the truth. I eventually released my mother and father from my anger since they are no longer alive for me to confront. However, I still struggle with “sister issues” that I carry around in my invisible backpack.

Connecting It

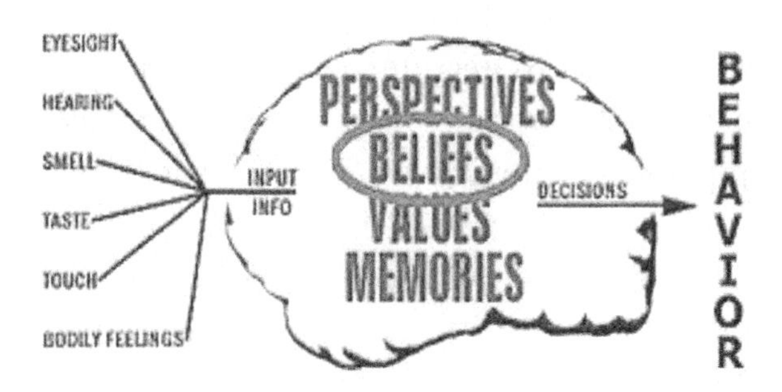

Events that happen in our lives create memories and shape our beliefs about the world and the people in it. They help us to determine our roles in life, how we think people should behave or treat us, and what we believe about ourselves. The beliefs we form based on our experiences are carried around in an invisible backpack. For students who were in foster care, their backpacks can be extremely heavy.

What's In The Invisible Backpack

Do you want to know what's in my backpack? Yes, I also have trust issues. How can I trust that anyone will have my back when the person whose God-given responsibility it was to be there to protect me and accept me for who I am, no matter what, let me down? Figure 11 illustrates some of the beliefs that foster youth have that impact their actions, view of the world and relationships with themselves and others.

Figure 11: The Invisible Backpack

Foster youth carry a heavy burden of guilt, shame, and misbeliefs caused by the complex trauma they have endured. These backpacks include beliefs about self and beliefs about others that become a reality and cause them to act in ways we may not understand. Let's look inside the invisible backpack.

Beliefs About Self

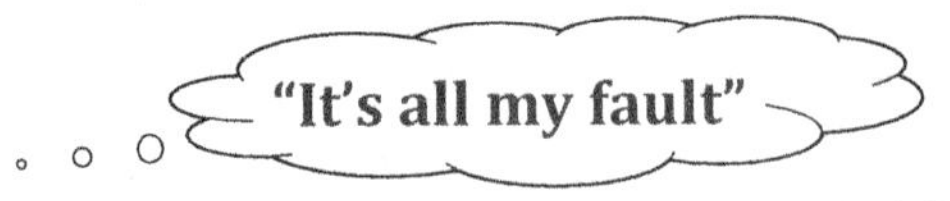

It may not make sense to you, but children carry guilt, self-blame, and shame about being in foster care. Depending upon the circumstance leading up to their abuse and removal, students may feel, "If I had not gotten in trouble, or been a better student, my parents would not have..." The truth is, there isn't anything less or more that a child could have done to control their parent's actions. Aside from self-imposed beliefs, a child may have been told by a family member that it was their fault, i.e., "If you hadn't told," or "If you had just obeyed," or "If you hadn't been around uncle so-and-so." These beliefs do not go away on their own.

One of the things you can do whenever you encounter a foster youth, is reassure them that being put in foster care is not their fault but the result of their parent's inability to provide a safe environment.

On average, by the time a foster child reaches high school they may have missed up to three years of school. Reasons for missed school days vary but may include:

- neglect of educational needs by parents
- court dates
- change in placements
- missing/incomplete academic records
- repeating courses
- lack of educational assessment

All these situations can be minimized. For our students, it doesn't feel like anyone is trying, so why should I?

Other factors which reinforce the belief, "I am stupid" may be:

- Foster youth are five times more likely to be placed in special education.
- Not receiving proper or any educational assessment.
- Repeating classes.
- Not getting proper credit for partial classes.
- The need for accommodations through Disabled Students Programs and Services or Special Services (depending upon the college)
- They have heard it from peers and parents.
- They struggle with learning disabilities.

While this may not be the truth, it feels like it is.
Many children think, "How can I feel loved when...?"

...My parent did not even want me around.

...I am being abused and hurt.

...I am being moved from home to home like I am on a world concert tour (without the fanfare).

...No one talks to me about all the changes going on with my case.

...I am labeled "unlovable" because of my behaviors when I am in survival mode.

...They only love me when I am "good". ...No one sticks around long enough to "work with me".

...No one is helping me to understand what is happening to my mind and body.

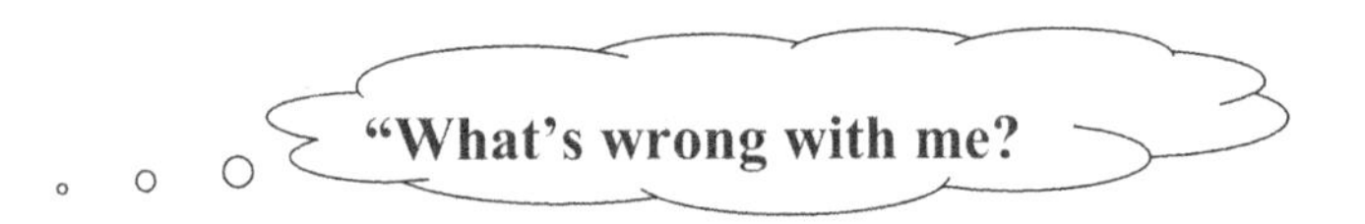

Some of the underlying thoughts based on actions by adults may include:

- There must be something wrong with me if my parents thought it was ok to hurt me or give me away.
- There are special programs, even at college, just for foster youth (it can be both a blessing and curse to be identified).
- I do not want to be wrong or different from everyone else.

"Different" and "wrong," are not synonymous. If it takes a little longer to grasp a concept, a student may need tutoring or accommodations for a disability. It does not mean something is "wrong" with them. Everyone occasionally needs some assistance. Do you wear glasses? Do you walk with a cane? Do you have someone else drive you around? If you answered "yes," to any of these questions, does it mean something is wrong with you? No, it just means that you need some assistance.

No one wants to feel like something is wrong with them or feel like they do not belong.

What can you do to help?

- Avoid engaging in the *What's Wrong Tango.*
- Encourage students to access resources by bringing the services to them or have them co-located in your center.

Beliefs About Others

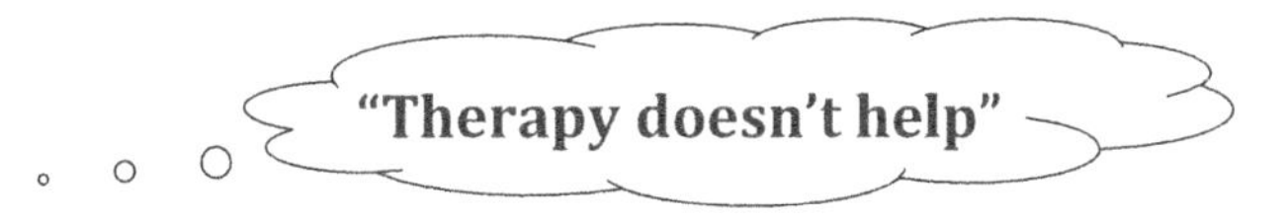

Too often our students' mental health treatment is relegated to interns who are usually on a one-year commitment. So, by the time a youth decides to open up, it is time for another therapist. This is another loss. If you were seeking therapy, would you not want to find someone with whom you connect and with whom you feel comfortable? Why should it be different for foster youth?

There is a lot of systemic change needed around the provision of mental health services for foster youth.

Here is a rundown of a typical therapy session:

> Therapist: "Hello Susie. Did you have a 'red', 'yellow', or 'green' day today?"
>
> Susie: "I don't know."
>
> Therapist: "Your caregiver tells me you had a 'red' day today. Let's see what we can do so you can have a 'yellow' day tomorrow and eventually all 'green' days."

This standard of therapy only addresses present behaviors at face value in an effort to make the behavior stop. This desire to stop a behavior is based on the needs of the adults who must deal with foster youth (e.g., caregivers, teachers, group home staff, or after school program staff). The adults want the calls from school, the fighting, and the destruction of property to stop.

Suggested Trauma-Informed Response

Encourage students to engage in trauma-informed therapy and interventions that will help them to recognize the lasting effects from their childhood traumatic experiences. The goal is to help youth to rethink how they respond to the triggers and reminders. The healing begins with helping them to distinguish between a perceived threat based on past patterns or an actual current threat to their physical, psychological, or emotional safety.

S

T

I

R

What can you do to help?

- Connect students to consistent trauma-focused therapy.
- Include mindfulness activities in your group meetings.
- Partner with community mental health providers to host sessions or workshops on campus
- Educate the campus community on effective ways to engage foster youth.
- Build relationships with the Department of Mental Health so you can assist students with advocating for services.

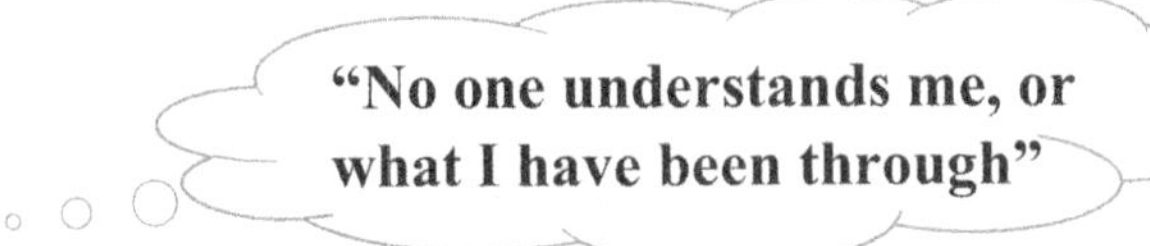

There are many well-intentioned adults touching the lives of our foster youth. Yet, it can be very isolating to be a student in foster care.

I conduct the training for potential volunteers who are interested in working with our students at either our K-12 or college sites. One of my goals is to dispel the "puppy syndrome." The "puppy syndrome" is where a bright-eyed, eager volunteer comes in with the notion that their mere presence is sufficient to change the life of a foster youth. Naively, they think it's like gifting the child a puppy. Their belief is, "I will be their puppy. Everyone likes puppies. Puppies are cute, cuddly, and playful". The truth is, not everyone likes puppies. Some people are allergic to them, some people are terrified of them, and still others prefer cats over dogs.

My goal is to share with potential volunteers some background into the experiences of our students and prepare them for the potentiality that not all students will gravitate to them. Trust and respect are not automatic but must be built over time. I also instruct them that it is not appropriate to ask students, "What happened?" or "How did you get into foster care?"

What can you do to help?

- Be careful not to say, "I understand."
- Create a space for students from foster care to build their own sense of community. This could include a designated space on campus, regular opportunities to come together, or even create a campus club.

We discussed Reactive Attachment Disorder (RAD) and the Cycle of Need/Attachment in a previous chapter. Once trust is broken by an adult who was responsible for helping to build trust during formative development, it doesn't just show up later because you as a professional think it should or because you say, "Trust me; I am trustworthy."

For foster youth, they have an external locus of control. The adults in their lives are making all the decisions "in their best interest", but no one is talking to them about it. Additionally, adults have made promises they did not keep. Social Workers have said, "If you do good in this home, I will arrange for visitation with your sibling." Some youth are still waiting for that visit.

Again, relationships are viewed as a contract. The belief is "No one helps just because. So, what do I need to do to get what I need from you?" This distrust also leads to the inability to delay gratification. Have you encountered a student who keeps bugging you about something you offered to them? Does this conversation sound familiar?

> You: "Meal vouchers are not ready yet. I will notify you when they are."
>
> Student: (Next day) "Hello. I just came by to see if the vouchers are ready yet."

The inability to delay gratification may look similar to signs of anxiety disorder.

What can you do to help?

- Do not make promises you cannot keep.
- Work with other departments to ensure they meet deadlines they have set.
- If there is a need for change, communicate that empathetically to students by approaching them before they need to come to you.

Applying It

Remember: everyone in the classroom has a story that leads to misbehavior or defiance. 9 times out of 10, the story behind the misbehavior won't make you angry. It will break your heart.

– Annette Breaux

Activity: Unpacking the Invisible Backpack

What are example behaviors you may see in your students that reinforce their beliefs about self?

Behavior #1:

____

____

Behavior #2:

____

____

Behavior #3:

____

____

What are things you can do within your program structure to counter these behaviors?

Action for Behavior #1: ________________________

____

____

Action for Behavior #2: ________________________

____

____

Action for Behavior #3: ________________________

____

____

4

Rewriting The Script: How You Can Help

"Anything that's human is mentionable, and anything that is mentionable can be more manageable. When we can talk about our feelings, they become less overwhelming, less upsetting, and less scary. The people we trust with that important talk can help us know that we are not alone." —***Fred Rogers***

This chapter will follow a slightly different format than the previous three chapters. I think you have mastered many definitions, so I would like to focus this chapter on connecting and applying the knowledge you have learned.

Connecting It

During a meeting for student equity, a manager asked, "Why do we need to focus on foster youth?" After getting over my annoyance with him for asking, I responded, "They are students like any other student who has the right to an education, but may need some extra supports to complete the journey." Further, foster youth account for approximately one percent of our total student population. A one percent differential in our transfer rates could make the difference in our ranking.

Missing Protective Factors

Many college-bound foster youth do not have all the foundational pieces needed to build the resiliency essential for college success. Of the seven factors noted in *Models and Theories of Student Success, Resilience and Well Being*, foster youth tend to be deficient in:

- the parent factor: characterized by strong and effective parenting
- the family and identity factor: where family identity and connectedness is evident
- the community factor: where the morals and values of the local community are transferred to the student

Being in a constant state of stress or survival mode decreases the neural connections in the brain so that learning is not taking place. Figure 12 illustrates the differences in the production of neural connections between a normal brain and a stressed brain.

Figure 12: Normal Brain Vs. Stressed Brain

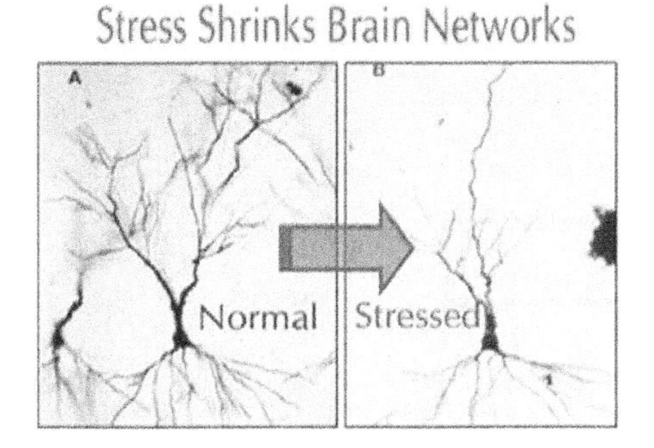

As you can see from the illustration of brain development, there are gaps in the stressed brain where neurons and connectors should be. So, foster youth who have suffered trauma and chronic stress are showing up at our colleges wanting to get an education (and having a right to do so), but their ability to learn and progress is diminished. These students need your assistance.

Helping Students

Our students have experienced distressing events with no reliable adult to help them make sense of what is happening. They come to you in an attempt to make connections and understand things that should have been explained to them long before they arrived at college.

In Dr. McKellar's paper "Information for Teachers", she highlights fostering supportive relationships and setting high expectations for students while providing meaningful opportunities for inclusion as key factors in building resiliency in students from foster care. No one lives up to zero expectations.

What can you do to help?

The To-Do List

- **Teach Executive Skills:** Create opportunities for your students to convene regularly in order to build a sense of community and inclusion. Plan workshops that cover topics such as time management, goal setting, problem solving, social etiquette and organization.

- **Build Resiliency**: Resiliency is 1) human capability to adapt and overcome risk and adversity; 2)the ability of individuals to rebuild their lives, even after devastating tragedies; 3)not something that you're either born with or without; 4) something that develops as people grow up and gain better ways of thinking, self-management skills, and more knowledge; 5) something that comes from supportive relationships

4 Acts to Resiliency

Here are some things I believe you can do. I call them the *4 Acts to Resiliency*. Encourage students to acknowledge, affirm, acquire, and attain:

- ***Acknowledge*** they have been hurt, but use the hurt as a catalyst to move ahead instead of a reason to remain behind.
- ***Affirm*** themselves. Help them to understand they are not their circumstances and encourage them to speak positive affirmations to themselves. "I know I am worthwhile." "It is safe for me to succeed." "I love and approve of myself." "I am loving and lovable."

- ***Acquire*** a support network. Find someone who is doing something positive and spend time with them.

- ***Attain*** their goals. Setting goals gives students something to look forward to and rejoice when they are achieved. "I now go beyond other people's fears and limitations." "I create my life."

The Not-To-Do List

- **Do Not Buy Into The Beliefs In The Invisible Backpack:** If a student's belief is, "There is something wrong with me", perhaps we should examine our messaging. Even if we are well-intentioned, the things that we do may isolate our students, or can backfire if we do not perform them correctly. Now that students know more about the benefits, it's not such a closemouthed situation. Do we really want to identify our students with these giant labels on backpacks and school paraphernalia that advertise our programs? "Hey, look at me. I am a DSPS or foster care student." This literal labeling can also be traumatizing. Being trauma-informed means being mindful of some of the things that we do when promoting student equity and access.

- **Do Not Take It Personally:** I would like to refer to one of the Four Agreements written by Don Miguel Ruiz, "Do not take anything personally." We are selfish beings by nature, and we have a way of slanting situations, so they have personal relevance or significance.

If a student says "you" are not helpful, they may be referring to the program or a decision you made based on policy which is outside of your control. It is not usually about you specifically.

When we take the behaviors and outcomes of our students personally, we get caught up in the trauma cycle.

Figure 13: Trauma Cycle

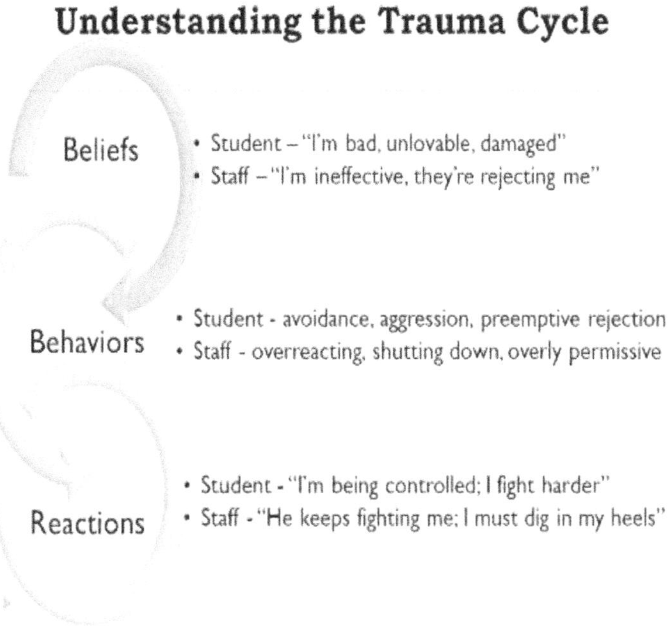

Understanding the Trauma Cycle

Beliefs
- Student – "I'm bad, unlovable, damaged"
- Staff – "I'm ineffective, they're rejecting me"

Behaviors
- Student - avoidance, aggression, preemptive rejection
- Staff - overreacting, shutting down, overly permissive

Reactions
- Student - "I'm being controlled; I fight harder"
- Staff - "He keeps fighting me; I must dig in my heels"

Helping the Program

I am aware there is not a "one size fits all" solution to creating programs. However, there are many publications that provide insight on structuring your program. Casey Family Programs authored *Supporting Success: Improving Higher Education Outcomes for Students from Foster Care* in 2010, for which I was a contributing college representative. The publication identifies the following core elements for a successful program:

- Designated leadership
- Internal and external champions
- Collaborations with community agencies
- Data-driven decision making
- Staff/peer support and professional development Sustainability planning

I would like to share with you a few lessons I learned after more than ten years of working with the program.

- Create a mission for the program. As you are adding staff, having a mission helps to keep everyone functioning as a team. Additionally, as staff transition in and out of the program, procedures are not recreated. Our students have already had many transitions; being consistent will avoid re-traumatization.
- Define roles clearly. Clearly defined roles can minimize duplicating efforts, overlooking

essential tasks, and creating feelings of being undervalued or overutilized.

- Meet regularly as a whole team. This helps with uniformity and allows policy updates to be shared simultaneously. Staff can also confer regarding student needs and successes. We should alleviate students' need to retell their story when extenuating circumstances arise. Additionally, you can address challenges before they become a crisis.
- Examine your policies and procedures. Are they trauma-informed? Could your processes inadvertently cause a student to be retraumatized?
- Provide training for new staff on trauma-informed engagement of foster youth.

Getting the Word Out

Many of you have seasoned programs and are providing excellent supports, but does anyone know about them?

- What are you doing to let students know you are available?
- Do you know who your students are on campus?
- How can you reach students in your K-12 district schools?
- What perception does your campus have of foster youth?

- Where can you find opportunities to share the support services available to foster youth with your campus community?
- Is there an opportunity to provide information to your Board of Trustees?

Developing Alliances

I am the queen of collaboration. My philosophy is why do it all by myself when there are many community agencies and campus programs that have similar missions? In my role as Director of Foster/Kinship Care Education, I am required to convene a quarterly advisory committee. As I am out in the community, I share the work we are doing at the college and find ways to collaborate.

- Who are your champions?
- Who in administration is an ally?
- Do you have a connection to your County Office of Education?
- Do you have contact with your K-12 District Foster Care Liaison?
- Which community agencies may be able to co-locate on campus to provide services to your students (i.e., Calfresh, the Independent Living Program or mental health provider)?
- Do you have a campus advisory committee or meet regularly with other Student Services Departments?

- Who are some of your potential philanthropic partners?
- Do you have a relationship with your campus food service vendor to provide meals for your students?

Helping Yourself

My hat is off to you as professionals working with and overseeing the foster youth support programs on your campus. Some of you are doing this work in addition to other assignments. Some schools have dedicated funds while others are piecing together multiple sources. No matter where you are in the process of developing your program, the work you do is greatly appreciated.

While I have thus far focused my attention on students, it is time to acknowledge you and the importance of being trauma-informed regarding your own self-care. I would like to remind you of two elements related to being trauma-informed:

- Realizing the widespread impact of trauma—you too can be impacted by trauma, either through personal circumstances or through the inadvertent trauma inflicted on you by students.
- Recognizing signs and symptoms of trauma in clients, families, staff, and others involved with the system. This includes recognizing trauma within yourself.

Let's check your trauma level:

Check Your Trauma Level	
Behavior	Yes/No
Are you having difficulty sleeping?	
Do you have trouble shutting out the stories of trauma shared by your students?	
Do you avoid students who have been verbally abusive to you?	
Do you find it difficult to listen to students' stories of challenge and childhood history?	

If you answered "yes" to any of these questions, you could be at risk for experiencing secondary stress injuries. These injuries are categorized as either compassion fatigue, secondary traumatic stress, or vicarious trauma.

Secondary Stress Injuries

The presence of symptoms of secondary stress injuries affects your empathy and compassion for others, which is the heart of what brings you into the helping profession.

Compassion Fatigue

Compassion fatigue, more specifically exhibited by those in the helping profession, is a form of emotional and physical exhaustion. It shows up as desensitization to student stories, higher rates of depression and anxiety disorders, stress leaves of absence, and degradation of the work environment.

This fatigue ultimately has an effect on your home life by decreasing empathy and the ability to connect to loved ones and friends.

Vicarious Trauma

Vicarious trauma affects those who engage empathetically with others who have experienced trauma. It results in a negative self-transformation characterized by alterations in spirituality or meaning and hope and manifests as the following changes:

Secondary Traumatic Stress

Secondary Traumatic stress can be triggered by listening to the horrific experiences of others. Your body internalizes what you may have heard and begins to react as if you actually lived through the event. Some of these reactions include hyperarousal, avoiding reminders or triggers, and even functional impairment.

Prolonged presence of symptoms may lead to a diagnosis of Post-traumatic Stress Disorder.

Self-care is Essential

It is not second nature for those in the helping professions to think of self-care. The focus is more on ensuring the well-being of others. Many have a negative connotation of self-care as being selfish. Yes, it is about being selfish but in a healthy way. If you are not careful to be kind to yourself and practice healthy habits, it will impact your ability to continue the work you have set as your career mission.

> **Food for thought:** You are a role model to the students you serve. While I know you are only human, you have placed yourself in position where you, unfortunately, are being held to a higher standard. If the students you are guiding discover that you are burnt out and not taking care of yourself, how might that impact their confidence, beliefs about self and others, and their hopes for overcoming life's challenges?

Celebrate Your Successes

What better way to heal from trauma than to recognize the positive outcomes you have achieved? This is also an opportunity to gather and share data.

- Have you seen an increase in the number of students coming to your office?
- Have you seen an increase in the number of students who transfer, receive certificates, or degrees?
- Do you convene your students regularly?
- Have you added new partnerships?
- Have you been able to offer more services over time, i.e., meals, books, or counselors?
- Have you seen a decrease in your drop-out rates?
- Has there been an increase in persistence, success, and retention rates?
- Have you increased your knowledge of foster youth and trauma-informed engagement?

Applying It

Trauma creates change you DON'T choose. Healing is about creating change you DO choose.

- Michelle Rosenthall

Activity: What's In Your Backpack?

What are your thoughts and beliefs about students in foster care?

____

____

____

How are you affected by working with students who have experienced trauma?

____

____

____

What are your beliefs about students with IEP's or disabilities?

____

____

____

What are your thoughts and beliefs about foster parents/caregivers?

____

____

____

What are your thoughts and beliefs about group home staff?____

____

____

What are your thoughts and beliefs about therapists?

____

____

____

What are your thoughts and beliefs about social workers?

____

____

Activity: Healing From Vicarious Trauma

Are You Leaving Yourself Vulnerable?	
Behavior	Yes/No
Do you rush heedlessly into stressful situations, then wonder why you feel overwhelmed?	
Do you take on a client/youth without thoughtful consideration of the ways our own issues interact with theirs, then wonder why we feel besieged?	
Do you take responsibility for things you can't control, then wonder why you feel out of control?	
Do you find it difficult to listen to students' stories of challenge and childhood history?	
Do you ignore the warning signs our bodies send us, then wonder why we get sick, develop back problems, overeat, or feel lethargic?	

Activity: Re-engage Your Senses

- When was the last time you took a break?
- Do you know what a rose really smells like?

Vicarious Trauma (VT) can cause your senses to become dull. The next time you take your break, think of ways you can be more mindful. Practice being mindful of the way things smell, how they feel, what they sound like, what they taste like, and what colors you see. For example, select a route you don't usually travel; notice what foliage is present and its colors and smells. What sounds do you hear along the route? When you go to the snack shop for a drink, notice the temperature of the beverage; is it too cold, too warm, or just right? What fruits do you taste specifically?

In Closing

If a book is well written, I always find it too short.

-Jane Austen

I do hope this quote from Jane Austen resonates with you after reading this book. *It's Not Drama, It's Trauma* was part of my healing process in understanding the drama that was recurring in my life and inhibiting me from having fulfilling relationships—even with myself. As I reflected on how my journey through foster care was impacting me in late adulthood, I wanted to share this revelation with others in hopes someone could benefit from the knowledge and help others who have experienced foster care.

Please remember there are reasons for every behavior. If you see a behavior as extreme or dramatic, take a moment to view it through your trauma lens and shift your mindset. I invite you to open yourself to empathetic trauma-informed engagement with everyone— including yourself.

Best wishes,

Theresa Reed

If you have found this book to be beneficial, please share it with others, or request a workshop. I welcome your feedback.

Website: www.INDITstore.com or www.TheresaReed.org
Email: **TheresaReed@outlook.com**

Like and follow me on social media:
@itsnotDramaitsTrauma or TheresaTraumaReed
@itsnotdramaits

Other Titles in the *It's Not Drama, It's Trauma* Series:

- *It's Not Drama, It's Trauma: Have You Considered it May Be Reactive Attachment Disorder or Oppositional Defiance Disorder?*
- *It's Not Drama, It's Trauma: Using Math As A Strategy For Trauma-Informed Engagement With Foster Youth And Other Children With Mental Illness.*
- *It's Not Drama, It's Trauma: From A Foster Youth To Foster Youth- There's Nothing Wrong With You, You Are F.I.N.E.*
- *It's Not Drama, It's Vicarious Trauma*

Bibliography

ACEs study. 14 June 2016. Document. 08 May 2018.

Bailey, Regina. Thought.com. Science, Tech, Math. What Does the Brain's Cerebral Cortex Do?

Casey Family Programs authored Supporting Success: Improving Higher Education Outcomes for Students from Foster Care

Children Now. *2014 California Children's Report Card*. Policy Report. Sacramento: Children Now, 2014. document.

Children's Bureau/ACYF/ACF/HHS . "Definitions of Child Abuse and Neglect." April 2016. *childwelfare.gov*. document. 10 May 2018.

McKellar, Nancy Ph.D. "Foster Care For Children: Information For Teachers." *National Association of School Psychologists* (2014): S229 to S2-32. handouts.

McKelvey, Cynthia. *MicNetwork, Inc.* 17 September 2015. article. 10 May 2018.

Mental Health America. *Self-injury (Cutting, Self-Harm or Self-Mutilation)*. 2018. web page. 8 May 2018.

Mental Health First Aid. "Myths and Facts About Suicide and Non-suicidal Self-Injury." *course material*. Washington DC: the National Council for Behavioral Health, 8 May 2015. document.

Merriam-Webster, Inc. *Learner's Dictionary*. 2018. webpage. 13 May 2018.

NCTSN. *Caring for Children Who Have Experienced Trauma: A Workshop for Resource Parents in their communities.* National Child Traumatic Stress Network, n.d. Manual.

Raburn, Stephen. *SpecialNeeds.com*. 2018. document. 8 May 2018.

Research, Center for Social Services. *CDSS 5A - Use of Psychotropic Medications*. 8 May 2018. <http://cssr.berkeley.edu/ucb_childwelfare/CDSS_5A.aspx>.

SAMHSA. *Mental Disorders*. 27 October 2015. web page. 8 May 2018.

Winch, Dr. Guy. *Salon.com*. 23 July 2013. article. 10 May 2018.

Cranney, J. and Andrews, A. The OLT Project *"Curriculum Renewal to Build Student Resilience and Success.*

Notes

Notes

Made in the USA
Las Vegas, NV
31 May 2024

90581035R00085